AF486353

The Corporation of NIL Sports

The Athlete to Entrepreneurship

Johnny Studstill Jr

© Copyright 2024 - All rights reserved.

The content contained within this book may not be reproduced, duplicated or transmitted without direct written permission from the author or the publisher.

Under no circumstances will any blame or legal responsibility be held against the publisher, or author, for any damages, reparation, or monetary loss due to the information contained within this book, either directly or indirectly.

Legal Notice:

This book is copyright protected. It is only for personal use. You cannot amend, distribute, sell, use, quote or paraphrase any part, or the content within this book, without the consent of the author or publisher.

Disclaimer Notice:

Please note the information contained within this document is for educational and entertainment purposes only. All effort has been executed to present accurate, up to date, reliable, complete information. No warranties of any kind are declared or implied. Readers acknowledge that the author is not engaged in the rendering of legal, financial, medical or professional advice. The content within this book has been derived from various sources. Please consult a licensed professional before attempting any techniques outlined in this book.

By reading this document, the reader agrees that under no circumstances is the author responsible for any losses, direct or indirect, that are incurred as a result of the use of the information contained within this document, including, but not limited to, errors, omissions, or inaccuracies.

Want More Reads Like This Or Readings About Entrepreneurship? Teens, Athletes & Entrepreneurs Visit StudstillCo Online Store by going to https://payhip.com/StudstillCo and click on "Join Our Mailing" to stay updated on exclusive consulting, special offers for new books and courses, and transformative insights. Don't miss out on the opportunity to be part of a community dedicated to innovation and cosmic exploration.

If you enjoy this book, can you give the author a review? Please visit www.amazon.com/author/johnnystudstilljr

Table of Contents

Introduction

In 2022, global sports market revenue stood at a whopping 403 billion USD, and by 2028, it's expected to be worth over 680 billion USD (Gough, 2024). In an industry ranking in that kind of money, only having athletic skills isn't anywhere close to enough, not if you want to turn sports into a secure, serious career. Sure, athletic skills open up the massive world of collegiate athletics for you, but being an athlete is only the beginning. There are more than 500,000 student-athletes like you training across U.S. colleges and universities (For student-athletes to succeed, 2024), and you don't need me to tell you that it's both a matter of pride and privilege to be a part of this fraternity. That being said, this privilege also comes with certain responsibilities.

As much as you'd give everything to get down on the field and play your heart out, it's also obvious that collegiate sports aren't all fun and games. The substantially large athlete community is governed by bodies such as the National Association of Intercollegiate Athletics (NAIA), the National Junior College Athletic Association (NJCAA), and by far the most influential National Collegiate Athletic Association (NCAA). Understanding NIL rights without getting a big-picture view of the NCAA would be like digging straight into desserts without having your meal. So, let's try to understand a little bit of the NCAA's history.

Where It All Began

The NCAA has a long history. Right from its inception in 1906 under the name Intercollegiate Athletic Association to its present form, this organization has undergone several changes. For instance, it wasn't until 1910 that it adopted its current name, and it wasn't until 1942 that it acquired the powerful position it has today in the field of intercollegiate sports (Britannica, 2024). The NCAA's influence extends to almost 24 sports in men's and women's categories, including football, basketball, baseball, lacrosse, soccer, ice hockey, and so on. In a nutshell, whichever sport you play, you want to be on top of NCAA regulations if you want to make true headway in your athletic career.

Staying true to its tradition of constant evolution, the NCAA came up with a new set of rules in 2021 that equipped athletes to use their *name, image, and likeness*, better known as NIL, to gain financial leverage in commercial contexts. Prior to this, while educational institutions, leagues, and the NCAA at large made millions and billions in revenue from the popularity of the athletes, the athletes themselves hardly had anything to show for it. Now, you might think that any sane person would see the unfairness of the pre-NIL arrangement, and yet the passing of these laws was anything but a straight and smooth journey, with several states passing the NIL laws in quite a staggered fashion.

Today, the NIL rights have completely flipped the game for all athletes. Student-athletes can now capitalize on their celebrity status in several ways, including signings, licensed merchandise, appearances, and endorsements. Of course, there may be certain limitations to these activities depending on where they're located. For instance, some state laws may ban athletes from endorsing tobacco and alcohol products, while others may restrict them from associating with activities such as gambling. For the longest time, the NCAA rules also prohibited what's popularly known as "pay-for-play," but recent developments (highly debated as they may be) suggest that this might be changing. More on that later, but for now, suffice it to say that effectively leveraging your NIL rights by staying within the limits defined by the NCAA can boost your career a great deal.

When the Going Gets Tough

As glamorous as the collegiate athletics world may seem from afar, it's not always rainbows and roses. Going in with a realistic view of the challenges you may face may just save you considerable stress and turmoil. These challenges can be broadly categorized as internal and external (Njororai Simiyu, 2010):

1. **Internal factors:** Think of these as ones that spring from personal aspects, and thus, you have much greater control over them.

    A. **Time constraints:** It's no secret that college athletes are pressed for time commitments on all sides. Training sessions, game schedules, academic assignments, tests, and even hanging out with friends must all be planned for in an athlete's daily routine. I've met several athletes who go in thinking that it'll all work itself out but are then so overwhelmed when they realize that time management is probably just as difficult and critical as learning a new skill related to their sport.

    B. **Career goals:** With all the above immediate short-term tasks taking up space in an athlete's mind, they may find themselves unable to plan for the equally crucial long-term career planning. I know what you're thinking, *But what's there to think about? Student-athletes are obviously planning to make a career in their respective sports, aren't they?* You'd be absolutely right, but (and it's a big but right there!) take a moment to think about how many student-athletes actually get drafted into professional leagues. It's quite a small percentage, to be honest. This means that even though the career progression of student-athletes seems straightforward, they also need the right career guidance so that they aren't left high and dry.

    C. **Grades:** Now, it's easy to get lost in the fancy career opportunities, the complicated NCAA intricacies, and the overall privileges and popularity that come with being a student-athlete. It's not uncommon for athletes to be treated differently by teachers, parents, and other students. For instance, teachers may grade them more generously; parents may prioritize matches over tests, and so on. However, at the end of the day, it's important to remember that the "student" part of being a student-athlete is just as crucial as the "athlete" part.

D. **Physical and emotional strain:** In addition to the tremendous physical demands that student-athletes are subject to, they often also suffer from significant emotional disturbances. These may not be extraordinary stressors but rather routine ones such as homesickness, coping with loss, and loneliness that all young adults must face now and then. Yet, they assume magnified importance when the athlete is already stretched physically and mentally.

2. **External factors:** As draining as the above factors are, they can still be managed with intervention strategies such as time management, appropriate guidance, counseling therapy, and so on. However, those aren't all the challenges student-athletes are faced with. A considerable amount of stress often comes from external factors that are outside their circle of control and yet can impact their wellness quite a bit.

   A. **Coach demands:** Every student-athlete knows that they'll probably be seeing their coaches more than their friends and family. While coaches are very well aware of the academic requirements that student-athletes must fulfill, they're often under tremendous pressure from educational institutions to bring in the trophies and rewards. It's not uncommon for these pressures to get displaced onto the athletes, creating strenuous and almost unrealistic schedules for them. Applying themselves in these stressful settings can turn out to be an extreme test of mental strength for the athletes.

   B. **Institutional policies:** Most institutes have set rules in place to account for student-athletes who have to miss classes when they travel for tournaments. However, these policies may not always be reflected in the attitudes of the faculty implementing them. Teaching and non-teaching staff may have disrespectful and discriminatory stereotypes regarding athletes, which impairs their empathetic capabilities toward these athletes. These stereotypes may even be worsened by racial and gender biases, creating an intense source of stress for the student-athlete.

Add to these the financial stressors that a student-athlete may have to face, and the sport itself may seem almost secondary to everything that's going on. Now, I want you to understand that the idea here isn't to discourage you from pursuing an athletic career. Not at all! On the contrary, it's to allow you to prepare yourself for the challenges that lie ahead. A major part of this preparation is to learn to leverage the existing laws, rules, and policies to your advantage, and the NIL rights can help you do exactly that!

Ready for the Transformation?

Good student-athletes have an efficient system to manage all of the above factors. Even when they cannot control external factors, they still have the right mental mechanisms in place that allow them to keep going. However, great student-athletes realize that the full utilization of their potential lies beyond this stress management and are able to add the NIL leverage to their athletic portfolio. So, if you want to be your best version, it's critical that you manage the stressors within you and your environment but also rise beyond those stressors to create a brand for yourself.

The name, image, and likeness (NIL) rules have ushered in a new era of empowered student-athletes. Many people wrongly assume that NIL is simply about endorsements. However, this couldn't be farther from the truth. NIL allows you to control your destiny by expanding your identity from a student-athlete to a "student-athlete-entrepreneur." I like to call this the "3I transformation:"

- **Income:** This one's obvious—the better your NIL game, the more financial opportunities you'll have. If some reports are to be believed, the NIL marketplace is valued at around $750 million to $1 billion, and this value is expected to increase to three to five billion by 2028 (Romboy, 2023). Those are big bucks, and you can have your fair share, too.

- **Influence:** NIL isn't just about financial opportunity; rather, it's about the ability to expand the student-athlete's influence. By creating your own brand presence, you have the potential to reach more people. After all, it's this influence that you have over your fan base that multiplies your endorsement opportunities, significantly increasing your return on investment (ROI).

- **Independence:** With the onset of NIL, the power dynamics have shifted drastically in favor of student-athletes. This paradigm shift allows you more independence and leverage when choosing the educational institution that offers you better opportunities.

Don't misunderstand me; the NIL rights, like everything else, have received criticism from certain quarters, but the advantages it offers you are too massive to be discarded. When you understand how these can boost your athletic journey, you become an invincible beast that never has to look back.

Don't take my word for it; just look at the success stories that abound in the sports landscape today. NIL rights have only been around for three years, and several student-athletes are already reaping the benefits. Take a look at On3's top five NIL valuations as reported on its website (NIL valuations and rankings, 2023):

1. Shedeur Sanders of the University of Colorado is valued at $4.6 million in football.

2. Livvy Dunne of Louisiana State University is valued at $3.9 million in gymnastics.

3. Bronny James of the University of Southern California is valued at $3.7 million in basketball.

4. Travis Hunter of the University of Colorado is valued at $2.7 million in football.

5. Arch Manning of the University of Texas is valued at $2.4 million in football.

If these figures don't nudge you to take your NIL rights more seriously, then nothing will. It's time to take charge and build your NIL identity, which gives you a brilliant edge over the competition.

This book delves into the step-by-step process of leveraging NIL to the maximum and untangling the complications along the way. Let me warn you, though: It's not always going to be easy. There will undoubtedly be ups and downs. The aspects we discuss in the coming pages may seem straightforward and even obvious enough on paper, but they may not always pan out in real life.

But then again, when has anything worth having ever been easy?! Your NIL brand won't be created overnight; it'll take persistence, patience, and consistency. You may even face technical hurdles, such as a lack of appropriate NCAA guidance or visa restrictions (for international students). The key is to have a clear vision and keep going while keeping your eyes on the prize. So, fasten that seatbelt and get ready for the rollercoaster ride ahead!

Chapter 1:

Building Your Brand

Your brand is what other people say about you when you're not in the room. –Jeff
Bezos

Do this for me: Close your eyes and think about your favorite celebrity.
What comes to mind? I bet it's not just their face that you thought
about. You likely also had a very clear image of the kind of work they
do, the clothes they wear, and in general, the way they carry themselves
in the public eye. For instance, when most people think of Steve Jobs,
they automatically associate Apple products and black turtlenecks with
him. The power of great branding lies in the fact that it's not aimed at
selling an isolated product but rather delivering an emotion-provoking
experience.

Even though branding may seem like an organizational exercise, the
above activity is a testament to how crucial it can be in your individual
journey, too. The problem is that most people don't start thinking
about their brands until much later in their journey. And when they do,
there's already so much past baggage left in their wake that building a
relatable brand becomes much more challenging. This isn't to say that
you must focus all your energy on the commercial aspects of your
student-athlete career. Not at all! At no point will your skills and
training assume a secondary position, and the notion that your hard
work will eventually shine is a fair one to a large extent. However, it's
critical to understand that optics matter in this day and age. If your
NIL brand can get you a one-way ticket to success-ville, then why not
make the most of it right from the beginning?

This chapter will break down the process of practical brand-building
into three parts, each with its own set of tips. Therefore, you can focus
on your game while building the right brand in easy steps. Dig in!

Step #1: Identifying Your Unique Value Proposition

Can you guess the most common response I get when I talk to athletes about branding themselves the right way? It's a thought that has probably crossed your mind too: *Isn't branding a little boastful? Almost like tooting your own horn?* The first thing to understand when building a successful brand is that it's NOT the same as delivering a rehearsed self-promotional pitch where you let go of all humility and boast about your accomplishments. The art of branding is a subtle one and consists of a much deeper approach than just blabbering about your achievements.

The first step is to identify your unique value proposition (UVP). I know that sounds like some fancy marketing jargon, but stay with me for a moment. A unique value proposition, popularly referred to as a unique selling point (USP), is nothing but what differentiates you from your competitors. Without this, you may never stand out in a crowd. Let's try to understand a product that I already mentioned, Apple. What makes Apple products stand out in a market flooded with smartphones from other brands? Well, it's the fact that the unique value proposition isn't centered around its latest tech features but rather the lifestyle of convenience, elegance, and functionality that it encourages its users to buy into. So, when you buy an Apple product, all those factors play into your experience rather than just the technology.

You may be wondering how this applies to your collegiate athletic career. The idea is simple—you are the product here, and the task is to figure out what unique aspects you can offer your target audience. This may seem simple enough on paper, but in truth, it requires a deep dive into who you are as a person *and* a student-athlete. Remember that this is an ongoing journey. You'll not arrive at a definite answer overnight, and even when you do, it may very well change as you evolve as a person over time.

Here are a few questions that can help you get started on the journey:

- **What are your values?** This refers to the guiding beliefs and attitudes that eventually determine your choices in life. Essentially, they reflect what you hold closest to your heart and what truly matters to you. For someone, it may be justice; for someone else, it may be courage; and for yet another person, it may be loyalty. You must figure out the values that dictate the decisions you make.

- **What are your needs?** This takes into account the goals you're trying to fulfill with your brand. You also want to have clarity in your mind about what needs are your top priorities and what would happen if one or more of these needs remained unfulfilled.

- **What are your interests and skills?** Think about which aspects of your student-athlete life you love to perform and also those that don't appeal to you as much.

- **What are your strengths?** It's crucial that you have a solid understanding of what you're good at and the areas that could use a little improvement. An individual may find that they're fantastic at problem-solving but not so great at research, and thus, your strengths and weaknesses have a considerable impact on whether your brand aligns with who you really are.

Your Brand as the Perfect Blend of Athletics and Business

One thing to remember when introspecting over these questions is that the responses must find a balance between your student-athlete identity and personal identity. This means that you need to go beyond your athletic values, needs, interests, and strengths. For instance, a star quarterback's leadership skills may very well help him build a close-knit, reliable team for a delivery service business.

Take a look at a few more examples of athletic traits that may prove extremely valuable when building a business brand for yourself:

- **Confidence:** The dedication to polishing their skills with constant training often gives many athletes a foundational sense of self. This kind of confidence and self-assurance may be especially valuable in the customer-facing aspects of building a brand.

- **Commitment:** Sports can be a fantastic character-building activity in itself that teaches you the value of physical and mental discipline. No matter how easy a successful brand makes it seem, you can be sure that it's like a duck, projecting a calm image on the surface and pedaling like crazy underwater. That kind of hustle is impossible without a deeply ingrained sense of commitment to seeing things through to completion.

- **Competitiveness:** Any kind of sport instills a deep desire to strive to be not only better than others but to always improve your own performance. This drive to achieve excellence rather than success can translate beautifully into a relentless pursuit of customer satisfaction.

- **Resilience:** Things don't always go your way on the field, but the ability to take it on the chin and move on can be a particularly valuable asset in managing business operations and supply chains, especially under adverse conditions. This also goes hand in hand with a growth mindset, which allows you to assess your failures as an opportunity to better yourself rather than as an obstacle that must be avoided at all costs.

- **Teamwork:** Team players tend to have an obvious edge in the business world solely because of their ability to tap into the shared potential of their teams rather than relying on their individual capabilities. This collaborative approach aiming for a win-win outcome can be especially crucial in conducting high-stake business negotiations.

- **Work ethic:** A strong work ethic is indispensable to building any business from scratch. It can come in very handy when establishing trust in the relationship-building phase of your business. After all, it's these trusting relationships that will create a strong foundation for your brand to be discovered by more people.

Of course, this is by no means an exhaustive list, and I highly recommend that you look within to determine which of your strengths can come in handy when engaging in brand-building.

Unveiling Your Strengths

If you have difficulty kickstarting the process, here's a nifty table for you to get started. Just put a checkmark next to the words that you relate to, and you'll have a comprehensive base that you can build upon gradually:

Strengths	Values	Interests and Skills	Needs
Delegation	Curiosity	Performing arts such as painting, music, dance, theater, etc.	Belonging
Organization	Judgment	Cooking / baking	Safety and security
Punctuality	Love of learning	Photography	Status and prestige
Problem-solving / analytical thinking	Perspective	Reading and research	Connection
Communication	Bravery	Gaming	Autonomy and

			control
Tech skills	Perseverance	Blogging/vlogging	Contribution to community
Resilience	Honesty	Gymming	Acceptance
Work ethic	Zest	Hiking	
Commitment and dedication	Love	Writing	
Competitive spirit	Kindness	Travel	
Creativity	Social intelligence	Pottery	
Confidence	Teamwork		
Multitasking	Fairness		
Taking initiative	Leadership		
Goal-setting	Forgiveness		
	Humility		
	Prudence		
	Self-regulation		
	Appreciation of beauty and excellence		

	Gratitude		
	Hope		
	Humor		
	Spirituality		
	Purpose		

The values column is derived from the values in action (VIA) inventory (The 24 character strengths, n.d.). The rest are words athletes frequently associate with themselves. My suggestion is: Don't get too wrapped up in the nomenclature of strengths, values, interests, and needs because there can be a significant overlap between those. Rather, focus on words that relate to you and that should give you a fair starting point for your introspective journey. Also, feel free to add to this list to customize it for yourself.

From a Student-Athlete to a Storyteller

Identifying your unique value proposition (UVP) is just the beginning of an adventurous quest you're about to embark upon. The next crucial step is to create your brand story cleverly centered around this UVP, and for this, you might have to put on your storytelling hat. An effective brand narrative doesn't happen by chance but requires deliberate efforts. Consider the following steps when leveraging your UVP to create the perfect brand story:

- **Step #1: Identify your target audience:** Imagine advertising the best steak restaurant to a group of vegans—no matter how great the steak, it just won't sell! That's why it's important to identify your target audience and create a brand that resonates with them. As an athlete, think about who you wish to inspire with your UVP and who'll relate most to it. Narrow down their demographics, such as age, sex, occupation, and socioeconomic background. Determine what section of the sports arena they occupy—are they fans, fellow athletes, coaches, sponsors, or some other population sector that can be commercially beneficial for you? Only when you align your target audience with your UVP will you be able to establish a clear direction for the brand you build.

- **Step #2: Craft a compelling story:** Once you've chosen your audience, it's time to tell them *why* they should care about you and your UVP. In his book, *Building a StoryBrand* (2017), Donald Miller outlines a fantastic blueprint for creating a brand story. According to him, successful brand stories have a hero (mind you, that's not you but your consumer) who faces a certain hurdle in achieving their goal and meets a guide who helps them overcome the problem with a plan and a call to action. *What does that even mean?* It means that no matter what your story is, the way you tell it can make or break your brand. For instance, if you're creating a brand for your fans, you need to understand that they aren't just celebrating your wins but rather visualizing themselves in a position where they can win too. They're essentially your fans because they see a little of themselves in you, and that's why they need to be the star of the narrative, not you. That's the difference between boasting about your achievements and strategically positioning your UVP.

- **Step #3: Choose the right look for your brand:** While it's essential that you choose a unique name that makes you stand out in a crowd, it's also critical that it stays in the "top of mind awareness" (TOMA) of your target audience. TOMA is frequently used in marketing to gauge how aware a consumer is of a particular brand. The higher the TOMA, the more likely your audience will purchase your product. So, the brand name must be both unique and easy enough to stay on top of the consumer's mind. Your brand logo can also help you in this pursuit. A large body of memory research offers evidence for what's known as the picture superiority effect, which means that people tend to remember pictures better than words (Ramaswamy, 2024). Think about it: What comes to mind when you see a big checkmark on a shoe? Additionally, you also want to ensure that the trademark for your chosen brand and logo isn't already taken, as this can cause serious legal hassle in the future.

- **Step #4: Optimize the audience engagement channel:** With your brand now all set to go, it's time to determine how you wish to interact with the audience you've worked so hard to identify. Setting up the right channels is extremely crucial for your brand. Social media is the best way to engage with your audience. Depending on the apps that your target segment frequents, open your accounts on all relevant platforms. We'll talk about creating an effective social media presence in just a while. For now, remember that though social media is critical, the value of having a professional website linked to your social media accounts cannot be overstated. You can do this yourself or get it done by a web design professional. Whatever the case, ensure that it matches your overall brand, not only in terms of visuals and color schemes but also the brand personality you're going for. The same goes for your social media accounts. This consistency in messaging creates a more uniform image in the minds of your audience and helps your brand remain in its TOMA more effectively.

- **Step #5: Create captivating content:** It's crucial to remember that creating a brand isn't a one-time event. Especially, in today's world, if your brand isn't showing up on your target segment's phone screens every once in a while, there's no way that you're going to be remembered. That doesn't mean you spam your audience. Much to the contrary, it's essential to curate a content strategy that resonates with your fan base. Consider sharing captivating and authentic pictures and posts that highlight your athletic achievements, behind-the-scenes moments at your games and events, or even your vulnerabilities at times. It's a good practice to ask yourself one question before every post: What is the purpose of this post—is it meant to entertain, connect, inspire, or educate? This will certainly help you avoid going overboard with your social media game.

Now that you know what goes into creating a solid brand, let's dig deeper into your social media presence that takes that brand to people.

Step #2: Building Your Social Media Presence

According to one report, before NIL rights were introduced, the then-freshman Paige Bueckers from the University of Connecticut women's basketball team could have earned $670,783 per year from endorsement posts shared with her huge social media following (Hodgkins, 2022). That's the power of social media to leverage your NIL rights. Even though almost everyone uses social media all the time, navigating it as a brand can be tricky and requires certain ground rules.

The first thing to note is that in branding, you aren't just doing it for fun. You must have clear, preset goals to ensure that you keep your eyes on the prize. A SMART goal-setting framework is often helpful here. SMART is an apt acronym for

- **S**pecific: It's time to kick out the vague objectives and make your goal as specific as possible. For instance, your goal may be to make one post daily to gain 1,000 followers in one month.

- **M**easurable: Quantifying your variables allows you to keep track of your progress.

- **A**chievable: While it's great to aim for the stars, it's also essential that you keep the goal realistic. This carves out a more precise path to success and avoids frustration and disappointment.

- **R**elevant: Ask yourself why you've set this goal. Does it make sense to you, or are you simply jumping on the bandwagon of other influencer statistics?

- **T**ime-bound: A goal without a definite timeline is like a football field without goalposts—you can run around all you want, but you aren't going to win.

When you set the right goals, you can leverage social media to bring tremendous benefits to your brand, from connecting with fans, promoting products, and showcasing athletic achievements to even networking and collaborating with others in the sports industry and outside. It's worth noting that the power of social media today is such that even traditional media houses and news channels often scope out the social media accounts of athletes to get their news stories. This means that if you crack the code of social media branding, you can take charge of the narrative that reaches your fans.

One of the most crucial aspects of cracking this code is choosing the right platform for your brand. What makes this tricky is that there's no one-size-fits-all solution, and many people fail at it because they end up wasting time on a platform that doesn't align with their target demographic. For instance, if you're targeting professional coaches who are typically in the older age range, then Snapchat may not be the best way to reach them; they may be more accessible on LinkedIn. On the other hand, younger fans use Snapchat much more prolifically.

In general, though, Meta (formerly known as Facebook), Instagram, X (formerly Twitter), and YouTube can give you a fair balance in the short and long-form content that helps you reach more diverse audiences, even within your demographic. For example, Instagram is great for visual short-form entertainment content, YouTube for longer educational and informative videos, and X for quick real-time updates on your events.

Crafting the Right Content Strategy

We already spoke about the importance of captivating content. Now, let's focus on specific tips that you can incorporate into your strategy:

1. **A posting schedule is critical:** In between your studies, training, and events, it's easy to forget to post once in a while. A frequent and consistent posting schedule is necessary to maintain the interest of your followers. Additionally, in the case of social media apps like Instagram, the more frequently you post, the higher your chances of being featured in the Explore feed or even among the top results for the keywords in your category. This greatly magnifies your reach. Along with this, you also want to experiment with the timing of your posts to

determine which time slots generate the most traffic. Remember that on many platforms, such as Meta, you can create a post and schedule it to be posted later. You can even use social media scheduling tools such as Post Planner, Feedly, and Planable to link your profiles across platforms and schedule your posts on all of them.

2. **Go for genuine, original content:** Aim for authentic, high-quality content because that's the primary user-facing aspect of your brand. If the content you post is carelessly written, contains a lot of fluff, has plagiarized elements, or is perceived as useless by your followers, they'll eventually stop trusting your brand entirely. Remember that the damage that badly posted content causes to your brand cannot be undone. So, think about what your target audience would prefer to watch or read about, and spend some time creating content specifically tailored to those preferences. You can get a fair sense of their preferences by doing a quick check of how certain past posts have performed statistically. Of course, this doesn't mean you post the same type of content over and over again, but finding a balance between variety and familiarity is key. When your audience notices that you put in effort to create such custom content, they're much more likely to feel connected to you.

3. **Understand the elements of posts:** Every post you make has very specific elements that you can use to your advantage.

   A. **Caption:** Research suggests that the most effective captions have about 138 to 150 characters in general and fewer than 125 characters for Instagram (Geyser, 2024). So, the trick is to keep it short and to the point.

   B. **Hashtags:** Hashtags aren't just strings of random words thrown together; they help you expand your reach and must be used strategically. Ensure that your posts have topical and relevant hashtags.

   C. **Image:** Keep your pictures high-quality and aligned with your brand image. Don't forget to fill in an accurate image description in the Alt (alternative) Text box. Screen-reading tools use this feature to describe the image to visually impaired users, and it's also great for the search engine optimization of your website.

    D. **Mentions:** Giving shoutouts to other accounts also helps increase your visibility a great deal.

    E. **Call to action:** Whenever possible, make sure you leave your followers with a specific call to action. It may be the usual "like, share, subscribe" request or inviting them to check out and try some of your endorsements. Either way, it contributes to audience engagement.

4. **Watch for the impact of algorithms:** It should come as no surprise that platform algorithms screen the majority of the content that reaches social media users today. Learning to leverage these algorithms is a big part of your social media journey. For instance, many social media platforms tend to prioritize visuals over written content, so adding relevant images or videos can boost your reach significantly.

5. **Engage with the audience:** Responding to people's comments or doing live streams where they can interact with you directly makes your brand accessible and relatable. When engaging in interactions, it's important to understand the difference between selling and overselling your brand. You want to ensure that your interactions aren't perceived as over-eager, desperate, or even intrusive.

Brand Engagement in Action

While everyone tells you to engage with your audience, it can get difficult to find the right medium of engagement. Sure, responding to comments is a great starting point, but the world of social media has a lot more opportunities to offer. Add to that the brilliantly diverse content you, as an athlete, can leverage, and you have a recipe for a blockbuster.

I already mentioned highlighting athletic achievements and taking your fans behind the scenes; here are a few more ideas to get you started on the brand engagement adventure:

1. **Start a challenge:** Challenge your fans to complete some of your training routines and post the videos. You can kickstart this by inviting fellow athletes, either from your sport or from other sports, to complete the challenge.

2. **Do "collabs":** Do collaborations with people from outside the sports industries. For instance, you can collaborate with a food vlogger exploring street foods or jam with a musician to show your non-athletic talents.

3. **Show the bloopers:** These behind-the-scenes posts have massive entertainment value and actually help people get over their assumption that athletes have superhuman abilities. So, don't be afraid to show them your epic fails on the field.

4. **Make then and now or before and after posts:** Every now and then, take a moment to appreciate how far you have come in your journey. Making posts highlighting how you have changed, either physically or mentally, can be quite inspiring for your followers.

5. **Talk about life as a student-athlete-entrepreneur:** Document the challenges you face balancing all these roles or the things that you love about performing these roles simultaneously. You may also share tips and advice for fellow student-athletes or aspiring athlete entrepreneurs, depending on your target demographic.

6. **Show your personal side once in a while:** The more your fans relate to you, the more they'll trust your brand. So, try showing them who you are outside the gaming arena. Let them see your vulnerabilities and doubts. Of course, you don't have to bare your heart publicly, but showing them your personal side can help you build a brand centered around your authentic self.

7. **Q&As:** Doing a question-and-answer round with your followers is one of the most popular engagement techniques and is used by even megastars such as Cristiano Ronaldo. You may also do polls and surveys on your posts from time to time.

Once you have a solid grip on your social media presence, it's time to move on to the third step of brand-building.

Step #3 Cultivating a Positive Public Image

Many people mistake a positive public image for a strong brand identity, but this is far from the truth. Remember that your brand image is the perception that you've successfully created in the minds of your audience. On the other hand, your public image refers to the trust and reputation that you earn with your real-time behavior. In other words, your brand image is what you want your demographic to believe about you, whereas your public image is what they deduce from your non-verbal and possibly non-curated attitudes and behaviors. For instance, an athlete who overcomes a serious injury earns the reputation of being perseverant, while someone who's caught cheating may be branded as unethical or immoral, even if it is an isolated instance. This reputation can have significant consequences for your brand, too.

Building a Positive Image

This image is especially important when you're just starting out, and people don't *know* you yet. This doesn't mean that you can throw caution to the wind in your later career, but as they say, first impressions matter. Ensure that you practice the following tips for a spotless public image:

- **Professional demeanor:** Regardless of whether yours is a formal or an informal brand, professional boundaries are a must. Note that professionalism isn't about showing up in a suit but goes far beyond that. Even when you try to relate to the younger crowds with fun and goofy content, it's important to remember that it's still business, and being presentable in that setting is of utmost importance. You may wonder, *"So what does it really mean to be professional, then?"* Consider incorporating the following traits in all your interactions and the content you post:

    A. Respectful

    B. Strong work ethic

    C. Honesty and integrity

    D. Articulate

    E. Well-groomed

- Many of these can prove tricky in an online setting, especially because most people don't take them as seriously as an offline meeting, for instance. But, as a student-athlete brand, you must present a professional front because, whether it's online or offline, unprofessional behavior can have serious consequences for your reputation and your brand.

- **Responsiveness:** While being flooded with likes, follows, and positive comments is a wonderful feeling, remember that the internet can also be a somewhat dark place with a whole lot of criticism and trolling. How you choose to respond to it or not respond to it is a big contributor to your reputation. Remember that some of the online criticism and feedback may be valid, and the rest may not be worth responding to at all. Determining how you respond to valid but negative comments from your followers says a lot about your openness to feedback. For instance, if someone has a genuine complaint or a concern about a product you're endorsing, you may want to take some time to vet those concerns and respond to their concerns. Of course, there's no blanket formula for these interactions because you'll have to determine the level of responsiveness on a case-by-case basis.

- **Positive attitude:** It's important to remember that people don't just remember what you say or do but rather how you make them feel. While the online world seems to love controversy, it's not possible to build a sustainable brand and reputation with it. This doesn't mean that you suppress any controversial or unpopular opinions, but it's important to be aware of the impact that these may have on your business. Also, it's worth mentioning that articulating your opinions in a respectful manner rather than ranting and rambling about them may earn you more respect and trust.

These may all seem like basic things that everyone knows and does, but brands often forget the basics in the hopes of building an empire. With these, you may not scale peaks of success overnight, but you'll certainly build a foundation for your brand that goes a long way in business.

Managing Your Online Reputation

Managing your online reputation is more than just responding or not responding to comments and trolls. The marketing industry takes online reputation management very seriously, and so should you because ignoring it can be disastrous for your brand. Take the example of Nestle's standoff with Greenpeace. In 2019, Greenpeace accused Nestle of harmful environmental practices in a video (Lyons, 2023). Instead of managing the problem head-on, Nestle had YouTube take down the video. This resulted in a major backlash on their public page, after which they had to shut it down for a while until things calmed down.

If you wish to avoid such online reputation disasters, you must have an online reputation management (ORM) strategy in place. This strategy consists of four kinds of channels:

1. Paid media is where you pay for your brand to be featured.

2. Earned media, where your brand is covered by a third party, such as a news channel, without payment.

3. Shared media is your social media content posted from either your own or others' accounts.

4. Owned media refers to your own website or other channels that you control.

However, before you utilize one or more of these, it's important to be thoroughly aware of how your brand is perceived online. Do a Google search to find out what people are saying about it, how they rate it, and what the criticisms are. A great way to do this is by setting up a Google alert for any mentions you receive. If you want a more targeted approach, you may even go for apps such as Brand Monitoring to keep tabs on what's said about you. The quicker you address these criticisms, the better it is.

Crisis Management Tips

The last aspect of developing a positive public image is to have a crisis management strategy. The biggest mistake most people make is to assume that nothing disastrous can ever happen to their brand. Unfortunately, a crisis can come knocking at the most unexpected times, more so in the virtual world, and you must be prepared to protect your reputation at all costs. With a strong ORM, you already have a strong grasp over quickly identifying the crisis of negative comments about your brand. However, how constructively you respond to these criticisms forms your crisis management strategy and often determines the outcome.

- **Step#1—Develop a plan:** Keep a protocol ready for when a crisis arises so that you don't get paralyzed with overwhelming emotions when there's trouble. Would you want to take off the problematic content? Would you like to communicate with the person posting criticisms? Is legal action on the cards? These may all be viable options, but you have to determine in which order you'd like to exhaust them. You also want to focus your energy on aspects that significantly impact your business, such as a bad review of your brand. On the other hand, a stray negative comment on your livestream may not require you to deploy any resources.

- **Step #2—Effective communication:** Once you identify a crisis that requires intervention, ensure you respond quickly and authentically. Remember that a defensive approach can lead to unnecessary escalations, so try to be as open, honest, and respectful as possible, even if the other party isn't being all those things. If you find that the problem is genuine, show your followers that you're working toward a solution, even though you may not have it right away. Also, keep your followers updated on the steps you've taken to fix the highlighted problem. Big companies often have ready-made response drafts or templates for common problems to save time, and you may consider this tactic, too, as your brand grows.

- **Step #3—Continued monitoring and assessment:** Effective crisis management will very likely be reflected in your data analysis. Keep tracking the up-moves as well as dips in variables such as traffic, number of followers, ratings, and reviews.

I know that it seems like we've been using a lot of marketing jargon here, but the reality of the matter is that branding is a marketing exercise. If you can use all of the above marketing concepts to your advantage, you'll undoubtedly have a strong headstart in your business. That being said, marketing and your brand are only useful when you have a solid business idea. The next chapter will provide you with tips and tricks for developing the perfect business idea.

Chapter 2

Discovering Your Business Idea

Handing a thirsty man an empty but beautifully handcrafted antique glass worth thousands of dollars is practically useless—the value of the glass doesn't quench his thirst. Similarly, a fantastic brand without a viable business idea is no use at all. While the brand is about people's perceptions, your business idea is all about the product you're trying to sell. It's important that you spend a significant amount of time developing a business idea that aligns with your skills, passions, and the target demographic that you've identified.

As important as your business idea is, successful businesses don't grow on trees. Several things must fall into place for an idea to blossom into a potentially good business. Think about it: Prior to the 1980s, no one could have imagined the existence of something like the Internet, and yet today, it has evolved to be an integral part of all our lives. The point is that, sure, there will be some "Eureka!" moments where the idea emerges fully formed in your mind. However, that's a rare occurrence. In most cases, arriving at a viable and profitable idea requires putting it through the stringent scrutiny of a defined process. This chapter divides the process of arriving at the perfect business idea into three steps: identifying market needs, capitalizing on your athletic experience, and exploring franchise and partnership opportunities.

Identifying Market Needs

Would you sell football gear to a gymnast or basketball to a baseball player? Silly question, isn't it? Well, that's all that identifying market needs really is. Any product or service, no matter how basic or complex, can take off only if it fulfills a market need by solving a problem for the target demographic. In other words, selling the best products to an inappropriate market will *always* end in failure.

When finding the perfect idea for your business, you want to look for three major traits: clear market demand, being scalable and profitable, and being aligned with your life vision. The key is to keep brainstorming ideas without judging or discarding them right away. The more ideas you brainstorm, the higher the chance of finding one that fulfills all three criteria. Remember, you don't have to always come up with brand new ideas either. There are plenty of great businesses out there (both locally and globally), and you may decide to just build off of one of those. This section is all about finding out what your target demographic is looking for and developing a business centered around that.

Market Research Basics

Market research begins with the simple act of keeping your eyes and ears open to assimilate all that's being said around you. What are people's most recent preferences? What are they consuming? Where are they hanging out? Who do they follow? These questions can be answered with mere observation. Though this is where it begins, it certainly doesn't end there. In the pursuit of building a serious business, you cannot wait for the vague possibility of stumbling upon something lucrative.

To build a successful business, you must follow a more structured approach that focuses on collecting data in a systematic manner and then interpreting it as objectively as possible. It's this meticulous and unbiased approach that will help you significantly lower the risk of your business decisions. Here are a few questions that market research can help you answer in your entrepreneurial journey:

- What's my target's problem, and what solutions are they looking for?

- What's the market size I'm looking at?

- What are the best ways to reach my target demographic?

- Who are my competitors?

- Which products does my target prefer, and at what price?

Market research can either be quantitative with numeric measures or qualitative, which focuses on exploring the concerns that come up rather than only quantifying them. You may decide to do this research on your own, resulting in primary data, or rely on the secondary data gathered by others. Remember that both of these sources, as well as both types of research, are equally important in developing the perfect idea that fits your demographic.

Even though market research seems like a complicated task, you can conduct your own, at least at a preliminary level, in a few easy steps:

- **Research competitors:** When you have an idea that fulfills the three primary criteria, it's time to move on to the next step. The first thing you want to do is to take a detailed look at all the possible competitors in that niche. The easiest way to do this is to conduct a quick Google search for your product or service and research the top results that pop up. There are also specialized websites like Product Hunt or Crunchbase, which may give you a more organized list of competitors in your category. Of course, this search is only the beginning. Once you have the primary list, it's time to do a deep dive into each of their profiles. Here are a few things you want to look for:

  A. The online experience that they offer

  B. Their reviews and ratings

  C. The problem areas in which the audience might be looking for solutions

  All of these are wonderful means of finding gaps in the market that you have the opportunity to fill with your business. You can make a spreadsheet with the following columns:

Competitor Name	Website	Social Media Profiles	Company / Product differentiator	Possible Improvements

Online tools such as SEMRush, SpyFu, Owletter, and BuzzSumo are some of the most popular and top-rated online tools that you can use for your competitor research.

- **Engage with your target audience:** An alternative way of gaining information on your competition is to ask the target demographic directly what products or services they use. This should tell you the importance of engaging with the audience. This can be done through surveys and questionnaires, interviews, or even focus groups. The goal is to understand the market as much as possible from the consumer's vantage point. A simple Google form touching upon the relevant questions can give you excellent data. The market research questions may be divided into four categories (Market research questions, 2022):

Demographics:	Product:
<ul><li>What's your age, gender, ethnicity, or marital status?</li><li>What's your educational qualification?</li><li>What is your monthly income range?</li><li>What methods of shopping do you prefer?</li><li>What's your shopping budget every month?</li></ul>	<ul><li>What do you best and least like about [the researched] product?</li><li>What problem does the product help you solve, and how?</li><li>How does our product compare with the other competitors'?</li><li>How does the product score on [price, customer</li></ul>

- How regularly do you shop for [the researched] product?	service, ease of use, etc.]? - What changes would you like to see in the product? - Does the product's value justify its market price? Is it in a range similar to its competitors? - How much would you pay for this product?
Customers: - How would you rate the product? - Why did you decide to use the product or service? - How does that fit your needs? - Would you recommend us to your friends? - Would you buy the product again? - How could we improve? - Why did you decide to buy the product from another brand? - How would you rate your	**Brand:** - How did you hear about us? What are people saying about our brand? - What do you think about our brand? - Do you follow us on social media platforms? - Did you check our reviews and testimonials before making the purchase? - When you think of our brand, what thoughts, aspirations, or emotions does it invoke? - Do you feel confident that you know what our brand

customer experience with us?	stands for?

Analyzing the responses from your audience using tools such as Excel, Google Sheets, or SPSS can bring you excellent insights about patterns that you may not have noticed before.

Making the Most of Emerging Trends in the Sports Industry

While market research gives you a broad playing field (pun intended!), it's important to note that the sports market today is as dynamic as the athletes who dominate it. This means that market trends change very frequently, and riding the right trend wave at the right time can prove extremely lucrative for your business. However, to squeeze out the profitability of trends, it's essential that you have a slightly futuristic orientation. Think about what trends the users find intriguing in the present and have the potential to blow up in the future. Here are the top three branding trends that may benefit your business:

- **Technology:** A survey of 700 global experts from various sections of the sports industry reports the use of technology, particularly AI and data analytics, as a common theme among the top trends impacting the industry (Ambler, 2024). Be it the integration of this technology into injury recovery programs or personalized training programs, technology plays a massive role in the evolution of sports today. Generative AI plays a major role in analyzing and predicting athletes' performance. If you're technologically inclined, this may be a great starting point for your product development. But what if tech products or services don't excite you? Well, it's still a fantastic idea to embrace this and other such upcoming technologies to boost your branding and marketing activities. For instance, today AI is helping big sports names such as the San Francisco Giants store, and manage their years' worth of data seamlessly. Even if you're just starting with your business, AI can still help you create customized content to expand your reach to those users who are most likely to opt for your brand.

- **Social impact:** In 2020, LeBron James and a few other popular African-American athletes formed a voting rights group to educate African-American citizens on their rights and responsibilities (Martin, 2024). While not all celebrities may choose to actively endorse social causes, it would be unwitting to assume that brands have no influence in this arena. Understand that with rising awareness, audiences are also becoming increasingly purpose-driven and expect their favorite brands to contribute to social change in some form. It's crucial to realize that you can create a sustainable, socially responsible, credible, and authentic brand without actually turning into a social activist. By embracing the social responsibility value that you bring to the table as an athlete, you can engage with global audiences on a far more organic level.

- **E-commerce:** The last trend that I want you to be mindful of is online retail. No matter what sport you play and what your business idea is, the increasingly user-friendly platforms with integrated AI features make it a very profitable opportunity. And more and more athletes are realizing this. Whether it's their branded merchandise, digital assets such as non-fungible tokens (NFTs), training courses, collectibles, or even exclusive content footage, athletes now have diverse ways of connecting with their fans while making a profit.

With these three critical trends in mind, let's now focus on some emerging trends in specific sports niches that may yield the perfect idea for your business: apparel, nutrition, and fitness.

1. **Apparel:**

    A. Women's sportswear, including yoga pants, running shorts, and so on

    B. Athleisure brands for both men and women

    C. Sports footwear

2. **Nutrition:**

    A. Energy drinks

    B. Protein powders

    C. Protein and energy bars

3. **Fitness:**

    A. Immersive or gamified fitness experiences

    B. Fitness wearables and devices

    C. Home fitness equipment

Looking Beyond Sports

While the sports industry is brimming with entrepreneurial opportunities, that's not all there is. Sure, that may be the first place you look, but don't forget that there is a whole world beyond sports, too. It's important to tap into skills outside of your sports potential. For instance, a student-athlete with a keen eye for fashion can consider launching a clothing line that is not centered solely around sportswear. Here are a few more ideas to consider:

- Being a nutritionist

- Starting a PR business

- Opening a gym

- Opening a restaurant/food-joint

- Being a talent scout

- Taking up photography

- Becoming an author

- Starting an affiliate business

The opportunities are endless; you only need to have a clear understanding of your interests, aptitudes, and life goals, and you'll find the perfect start-up for yourself.

Capitalizing on Your Athletic Experience

People often think of sports only in terms of either a hobby or a career, but the truth is that your athletic experience is a big part of who you are. And this is regardless of whether you choose to be an athlete or not. Your athletic experience has undoubtedly cultivated a set of unique skills within you that can prove critical when starting a business of your own. We already looked at your strengths and values in the first chapter, but let's take a moment to identify the transferable skills that you've developed thanks specifically to your sports training:

- **Coachability:** No matter how much research you do and how good your product and brand are, there will always be things that you don't know yet. Being open to and implementing relevant feedback is critical when building your business. As an athlete, you have the great advantage of screening random criticisms from valuable constructive feedback, and that's surely an asset.

- **Teamwork:** No matter what your business is, one thing you can be sure of is that you cannot do it all alone. In the beginning, you may lean on your friends and family for support, but eventually, as an entrepreneur, you'll have to hire a professional team working toward ultra-specific targets. It's at this stage in your business development that the importance of teamwork, group communication, and coordination skills from your athletic experience will be greatly magnified.

- **Time management:** Athletes, especially student-athletes, are no strangers to having too many things on their plates. As we saw earlier, they often have to strike the perfect balance between several responsibilities. Additionally, athletes understand the value of every single moment. They're well aware that it can end up being the difference between winning or losing a game. Entrepreneurship isn't much different, as you must adapt to market changes very frequently. If you are to do this successfully, you must have a solid grip on the management of tasks that consume your time. Your athletic experience can provide valuable insights in this regard, and we shall discuss this in detail a little later.

- **Decision-making under pressure:** Entrepreneurs and athletes both regularly face decision-making dilemmas that can make or break the ultimate output. Very often, it's not only about how effective the decision is but also how quickly it's arrived at. Having made such split-second choices on the field, you're much better equipped than your non-athletic counterparts to assess the available options and arrive at the most appropriate one.

- **Learning from failure:** Coming from an athletic background, you've undoubtedly seen what failure looks and feels like at close quarters. However, you also know that success is impossible without stumbling upon failure every now and then. Your athletic training promotes a growth mindset, which in turn allows you to see failure as an opportunity to learn what *not* to do. This mindset is critical in your entrepreneurial journey, which you'll find riddled with innocent and unsuspecting errors. Rather than letting them get you down, it's much more beneficial to allow them to improve your brand.

- **Goal-oriented competitiveness:** Athletes tend to be trained to be goal-achieving machines that prioritize SMART goal-setting. The SMART framework requires that the goals be specific, measurable, achievable, relevant, and time-bound. These quantified goals encourage a sense of healthy competition that's focused on a definite vision of the future and also a strong work ethic that prioritizes these goals over short-term gratification. This is again an invaluable trait for an aspiring entrepreneur.

Remember that by no means is this an exhaustive list of athletic characteristics that contribute to a successful entrepreneurial venture. Now, let's try to explore the virtues that you've received from your athletic experience.

Finding Your Niche

With all the brand-building tips we discussed earlier, you should be fairly confident about the general industry in which you'd like to establish your business. However, that's just the beginning; now it's time to find a specific niche where your unique athletic experiences and traits can be your trusted companion. Try out the following activity to uncover these traits for wonderful leverage in your business. Remember the traits you identified in the first chapter, as they may appear here too.

The **STAR method** is often helpful in articulating those skills that you may not have thought about previously. Interviewees are often encouraged to use this method when answering questions about their accomplishments. Here, however, this method will help you crystallize the skills for yourself. Think of specific achievements, such as winning a championship or overcoming a difficult injury, and try to answer the questions in the following table:

With these examples, you would have identified leadership, discipline as your strengths, strengths-based training of your teammates, and nutritional expertise as the skills that you may want to center your business niche around. A great business idea, in this case, would be to start a business focused on nutritional consultation or personalized agility training.

Exploring Franchise and Partnership Opportunities

In today's age, where you can find a McDonald's to eat at no matter which country you are in, the brilliant potential of investing in a franchise is no secret. Thanks to the strengths and transferable skills we've spoken about till now, franchises offer excellent opportunities for athlete entrepreneurs to take the next step toward becoming smart investors. These opportunities come with significant advantages for both parties. The franchisors can expand their business without incurring massive costs. On the other hand, the franchisees, or athlete-entrepreneurs in our case, can make profits with reduced risks due to the already tried and tested business models.

As great as franchises are, several factors determine whether they're the right fit for you. Take a look at a few that can help you evaluate if investing in a franchise would be a good idea:

- **Initial purchase costs:** Franchise fees are the initial investment that allows you to purchase the right to use the franchisor's name and business protocols. Franchisors may also charge some extra fees for training employees.

- **Ongoing fees:** In addition to the up-front fees, you also must pay ongoing royalty fees as a predetermined percentage of your sales.

- **Franchise background:** Before investing, it's imperative that you research the franchisor's track record of success and the competition that you may face. It's also essential that you carefully review the legal documents, such as franchise disclosure, to ensure you're on the right track.

- **Brand alignment:** As mentioned before, the NIL rules prohibit athletes from endorsing substances such as alcohol and tobacco. But even apart from this, you must be aware of the alignment between your athletic brand and the franchise.

For instance, a student-athlete brand focused on healthy nutrition wouldn't want to invest in a fast food franchise.

After evaluating these factors, if you feel a franchise is not the right path for you, then don't worry—you still have the option of considering a brand partnership. Such athlete-brand partnerships have become a popular marketing exercise, and rightly so. Established brands are onboarding more and more athletes to maximize their reach. Again, much like the franchise model, here too, both the brand and the athlete can reap the benefits. While the brand benefits from the athlete's popularity, the athlete can strengthen their market presence with resources that may not be available to them otherwise.

As in the case of franchises, brand partnerships also require that the partners you choose align with your brand and vision. For instance, you may be offered the opportunity to partner with local or even global giants in footwear, sportswear, nutritional supplements, and so on, but the one you choose will depend on your target audience and business goals. Thus, being aware of your own brand is critical at every step of the way. Once you've identified and developed the business idea and the business model that you wish to pursue, it's now time to understand the precise *how* of it all.

Chapter 3:

Developing Your Business Plan

Becoming an entrepreneur requires a solid understanding of this one fact: Ideas cannot become successful businesses until they're clearly quantified and crystallized on paper. To a layperson, this may seem like an unimportant detail to fuss over—as long as you have a great idea, what does it matter, right? But seasoned entrepreneurs know that without a properly structured plan for your business, it's way too easy to get lost.

No matter how popular you are as an athlete, you won't find finances for your business simply based on this popularity. Sure, popularity and branding are big factors, but for your business to be taken seriously, you must draft a business plan with the right core elements that tell prospective partners and investors all they need to know. This is the most effective tool that you can use to convince others that working with you would be in their best professional interests. This chapter will give you an insight into drafting the perfect business plan, which will be critical in your transformation from student-athlete to student-athlete-entrepreneur.

Getting the Core Elements Right

A study conducted by the University of Tennessee reports that 44% of new businesses shut shop within the first three years, whereas the Bureau of Labor Statistics suggests that 20% of small businesses close down in their first year and 50% by their fifth year (Simplilearn, 2024). Though these say nothing about sports and athlete businesses in particular, they're still pretty bleak figures. Of course, the purpose here isn't to scare you out of starting your business. Rather, it is to help you understand the fierce competition that awaits startups. Considering this, it becomes crucial that you put your best foot forward when setting up your venture, and a detailed, accurate business plan is the central piece of that puzzle.

Essentially, a business plan contains four core elements:

- Executive Summary

- Market Analysis

- Marketing Strategy

- Financial Projections

Let's look at each of these in detail.

Executive Summary

I meet several new athlete-entrepreneurs who are so excited to talk about their businesses that they hardly ever realize they've lost the person they're speaking to. Unfortunately, if this happens at the beginning of a business pitch, it can cause irreparable damage. This is where the executive summary comes into the picture.

An executive summary gives the reader a brief overview of the entire business plan. This overview is meant to capture the attention of the reader while giving them all the relevant information they need to make their decision. This summary is often confused with aspects such as the company description, business objectives, and even the vision and mission statements. While your business plan may include all of these, it isn't limited to them. So, how would you go about writing a succinct executive summary?

This document may be one or two pages long, but the specific length would depend on your business niche and industry. But no matter what niche you've chosen, it must contain certain aspects:

- **Introduction:** This gives a brief account of what is included in this summary.

- **Company overview:** Here, you have the opportunity to introduce your company to the reader. Take a moment to talk about your mission statement, emphasizing the vision, values, and purpose. This describes your brand's core identity and provides a sense of direction for moving forward. Here, you'll also focus on the growth opportunities you see in the near future.

- **Market summary:** The next aspect to tackle is the brief market overview. Here, you'll talk about the industry you're about to enter, the niche, and the demographic you're planning to target. You don't have to delve into too many details, but be sure to let the reader know the most important points.

- **Competitive edge:** Ensure that you highlight your unique value proposition, which acts as a differentiator in an impactful manner. Let the reader know exactly why you'll stand out even in a market crowded with competition.

- **Management and operations:** Here, talk briefly about the personnel you're planning to hire and categorize them into leadership and other positions. Also, talk about their key roles and responsibilities.

- **Marketing plan:** Mention the marketing strategies you plan to deploy for the product in the market. So, you'd talk about how you plan to reach the target audience you've identified.

- **Financial projections:** This is one of the most important aspects of the executive summary that will determine whether your readers continue to be interested. This doesn't mean that you need to fudge numbers to lead people into believing that your business is worth investing in. Absolutely not! Instead, give them clarity on how long it will be until the business breaks even and eventually starts making profits. Also, give them a brief overview of the company's overall finances and the existing assets and liabilities.

While these pointers can be somewhat technically overwhelming, their presence doesn't mean that the executive summary has to be dull and drab. Here are a few tips that you can follow so that the document doesn't lose its essence:

- **Tell your story:** Sure, figures and visuals are crucial, but potential investors and partners want to know you as an athlete-entrepreneur and your proposed business in its entirety. Don't be afraid to let your passion shine by talking about what matters to your business and how you plan to achieve it.

- **Focus on the important details:** The executive summary isn't the place to ramble on about your achievements. Ensure that you're brief and highlight the important details. Try to include research findings that support your financial and marketing projections.

- **Check your tone:** Be mindful of who the audience for your business plan is—are you pitching to a potential investor, a partner, or someone else? Remember that you'll need to tweak the plan depending on the audience. Ensure that your tone is accessible and yet exhibits authority, clarity, professionalism, and credibility. Try to stay away from cliche words and phrases such as "synergy," "cutting-edge technology," and so on.

Though this section appears first in your business plan, ensure that you write the entire business plan before writing the summary. This minimizes the chances of miscommunication and inconsistencies.

Market Analysis

Market analysis is the critical component that allows you to approximate how the target demographic will respond to your product. This requires that you do a deep dive into the target market and your competitors. Here, you'd approach the market both quantitatively and qualitatively. The quantitative aspects would track such things as market size and preferred prices, whereas the qualitative aspects would focus on your target's motives, aspirations, and values. There's no doubt that, apart from helping you tailor products to your audience, this market analysis also plays a crucial role in differentiating your brand and reducing your business risks. Therefore, it pays to have a structured, step-by-step approach for carrying out this analysis. Take a look at the following steps and the questions you need to answer at each step (Coursera, 2024).

Step #1: Industry research:

- What statistical data is available about your business industry and niche? Is there anything available on metrics such as revenue generated and industry standards?

- How many businesses are functional in this industry? How are the business fundamentals of these businesses?

- How big is the target demographic?

- What macroeconomic factors (government policies, laws, world events, etc.) impact the industry at large?

Step #2: Competitor research:

- What brands are the biggest trend-setters in the industry?

- What are their unique value propositions?

- How do the customers perceive them, as seen in their reviews and ratings?

- What content, social media, and marketing strategies do your competitors use to engage with the audience?

Step #3: Gap identification:

- How is your competition falling short in meeting consumer demands?

- How will your product fill the gap?

- What challenges could come your way in developing better products?

Step #4: Target market definition:

- What does a typical consumer look like to you? What's their age, gender, location, economic and educational backgrounds, and so on?

- What are their everyday routines like?

- What are their challenges and aspirations?

- What kind of vocabulary do they use to describe these desires and difficulties?

Step #5: Barrier recognition:

- What legal requirements must new businesses fulfill?

- What's the general cost of launching a business in this industry?

- What are the advertising and marketing costs of your competition?

Step #6: Sales forecast

- What specific products are you planning to sell?

- What are the manufacturing and distribution costs?

- Based on your target market, how much do you hope to sell?

- What prices are you planning to launch your products at?

Though step four is a great starting point to identify your target, the entire process of market analysis rests on detailed market segmentation. Therefore, it's only logical to do a comprehensive walk-through of how you'd do it.

Defining Your Target Customer

There's bound to be considerable variation, even within your target demographic. For instance, college football fans from Texas may have very different lifestyle preferences compared to those from Oregon. So, selling the same products and services to both these groups may not make sense. This is where market segmentation can help tremendously.

Market segmentation is the process of arriving at a more specific and limited version of the target demographic that you've already identified. The aim here is to identify the most profitable segments for your business idea. Segmentation can be of different types:

- **Demographic:** This takes into consideration factors such as age, gender, income, and education.

- **Geographic:** This one's obviously based on the location of the consumers, not just the states they belong to but even smaller segments such as neighborhoods, towns, and cities.

- **Behavioral:** Here, you group your potential customers based on the similarities in their behaviors. For instance, what kind of sports gear do they purchase and how often? How often do they watch games on TV or live in stadiums?

- **Benefit:** Remember how we spoke about narrowing the purpose of your brand? Benefit segmentation allows you to group your audiences according to the benefit they derive— entertainment, information, social connection, or inspiration— from your brand.

- **Loyalty:** In this kind of segmentation, you attempt to divide the demographic based on their loyalties to leagues, teams, or brands.

- **Psychographic:** This takes into account psychological factors such as lifestyle, beliefs, values, interests, and personality.

Let's say an athlete-entrepreneur partners with a media channel to create an e-sports streaming platform. Their first step would be to gather as much data as possible on all the above aspects. Then they could divide their prospective markets into several possible segments, such as the following:

- **Segment #1:** Younger casual football viewers living in New York City, maybe between ages 18 and 27, who live alone, without a lot of money to spare for their sports-related hobbies and expenses.

- **Segment #2:** Middle-aged hardcore football viewers, maybe between ages 28 and 45 years old, with stable high incomes who live with their families and don't mind taking a streaming subscription.

- **Segment #3:** Older viewers above 50 who have the income but are unwilling to spend on a tech product due to unfamiliarity.

Now, your market research and segmentation make it obvious that you can either create a profitable product solely for the second segment or may need to take a diversified approach for all three. For the first segment, you may think of introducing a pay-per-view product, whereas the third segment would take a much more time and effort-intensive effort of demand creation by educating the older viewers. These insights can be extremely crucial when launching a new product or service.

Identifying Your Competition

When you conduct your market research, you'll realize that not only does your customer base vary, but your competition is also significantly diverse. Whatever the product, you likely will be competing with other athletes and sports brands for the customer's attention. However, with a comprehensive analysis of their marketing strategy, you can carve out a unique niche for yourself.

It's important to recognize that there are two kinds of competition: direct and indirect. Direct competitors sell the same products as your brand, whereas indirect competitors may not sell the same products and services but are competing for the same customers in the online world. Till now, we've touched upon assessing your direct competition by reviewing their websites, content strategy, and customer feedback. A fantastic source for this may be to check online communities and forums that let you get the lay of the land authentically. However, even apart from this, you may want to check out a few more methods of identifying indirect competition:

- **Keyword search:** Indirect competition is centered around the idea that you are not only in competition with brands of other athletes that are in the same niche but with every other online resource that uses keywords similar to yours. This often comes under the heading of search engine optimization (SEO) strategy, which is an elaborate topic in itself. But for our purposes, let's just say that understanding what keywords your competition is using can give your market analysis a whole new layer. Free platforms such as Google Keyword Planner and paid ones such as Ahrefs and SEMRush can give you great insight into the websites (aka your competitors) that rank for keywords relevant to you.

- **Google results analysis:** The online presence of your brand has a lot to do with where you appear on search engines such as Google. After all, today, the first thing that anyone does when they come across something new is to search for it online. For every keyword search, search engines screen thousands of hits across the internet. Think about how many times you have checked out the results on the second page of Google results, and you'll understand how important it is to rank on the first page. To appear in the top results, you must understand which of your competitors are currently placed there. Analyzing the search engine results page (SERP) is one of the most effective ways of tailoring a content strategy around relevant keywords.

- **Paid data research:** Another extremely useful tool for identifying digital competition for your brand is Google Ads (formerly known as Adwords). You can head to this tool and search for keywords relevant to your business, and it gives you an insight into who's purchasing ads for those keywords. You may find that brands and websites paying for these keywords may never have popped up in your other analysis, but they are just as important to know.

The data received from all of these research methods can sometimes be overwhelming, especially when you discover that several athlete brands are competing for the same consumers. However, this is the time to remember the unique value proposition that you bring to your target audience and position it most appealingly. This requires a strong yet subtle marketing strategy.

Marketing Strategy

When you immerse yourself in your own branding and market research, you'll become more sensitive to the fact that marketing is, in fact, all around you all the time. Brands, regardless of their niche, are trying to get you to purchase their products everywhere. Right from the billboards to where on the grocery store shelves the products are placed, these are all marketing strategies in action. And if you want to win this game, you must adopt the right marketing strategy, too.

We covered the first part of designing this strategy when we discussed market segmentation, which allows you to take a targeted marketing approach. However, there are a few more aspects you want to familiarize yourself with. You'll often hear the phrase "marketing mix" in this regard, which focuses on the four Ps: product, price, place, and promotion.

Product

This refers to the product or service you're offering your consumers. It helps to categorize the product into three categories: The three categories are: the core product, which is what the customer is looking for; the actual product, which is the tangible product you're selling; and the augmented product, which gives added value to the audiences beyond the products. A crucial part of clarifying this distinction is to get your product or market fit right with the product questions we discussed in the last chapter. In addition to the product/market fit, your product strategy must also take into consideration other factors:

- **Budget:** How much money can you invest in product development, marketing, and distribution?

- **Personnel:** How many people do you have on your team to dedicate time to product development?

- **Time:** What's the product development and launch timeline you're looking at?

Price

The price at which you sell your product may depend on several factors, such as the cost of production, the demand for the product, and the competition. Remember that price is not just a figure but also how people decide whether your product is worth it. So, how do you go about setting this price, which could make or break your business? There are a few strategies you can choose from:

- **Cost-plus pricing:** This strategy takes into account the simple calculations of your costs, break-even point, and the markup you need to be profitable.

- **Competitive pricing:** This pricing strategy is all about adjusting your prices according to the prices offered by your competition. You can either be cooperative where you match the competitor's prices, aggressive where you keep the prices the same even when your competitors raise the prices, or dismissive where you pay no attention to what the competition is doing and offer your product at a premium price.

- **Price skimming:** If you have the first-mover advantage in a particular niche, *i.e.*, yours is an innovative product in the market, then you may even launch the product at a higher price and then lower it over time.

- **Penetration pricing:** This is when you try to make a space for yourself in a new market by positioning your product as cheaper and more affordable as compared to your competitors.

- **Value-based pricing:** This pricing strategy understands that the lowest price isn't always the most appealing feature of a product for a customer. Here, you'd instead focus on matching the price of your product to its perceived value.

Place

This takes into account the places in which you plan to sell your product. Do you wish to sell through physical channels such as stadiums and brick-and-mortar stores, e-commerce stores, or both? As straightforward as this decision may seem, there are a few things you need to consider when deciding your place strategy in the marketing mix:

- **Location:** The location you choose to sell in has tremendous implications not only for your sales but also for your brand. For instance, if you're selling a luxury experience, placing it on a Costco shelf may confuse your audience and hamper their value perception of your product.

- **Kind of distribution:** You must also decide whether direct or indirect distribution channels will be in your product's best interest. Do you take the direct channel, where you take on the responsibility of manufacturing your own product and also delivering it to the consumer? Or would you want to onboard a distributor to get the product to its final destination? Remember, while the first one gives you much greater control, it also requires a higher financial investment. On the other hand, the second option means you have to deal with several intermediaries, which can impact delivery timelines for the customer.

- **Channel exclusivity:** Whether you opt for exclusive distribution channels depends on your product category. Commodity products such as nutritional supplements may need intensive distribution channels to meet the high and consistent demand, whereas premium products may find an exclusive and limited distribution strategy adequate.

Promotion

This P is all about the specific tactics you use to sell the products, including advertising strategies, promotional appearances, sponsorships, content and social media marketing, and personal relations. Here are a few ways that you can leverage the promotional strategy:

- **Paid advertising:** Exploring paid, targeted advertising on social media platforms can generate excellent traffic for your website while also peaking product demand. You might want to look into Google Ads, Amazon Ads, and even Instagram and Facebook ads.

- **Content marketing:** The idea behind content marketing is to leverage the content that's aligned with your brand, which not only provides useful content but also gives them a sneak peek into what the brand is all about. Let's say your brand is about nutritional supplements. Your content strategy cannot be centered only around your brand. Instead, you may well create content about diet or the challenges that your audience faces when incorporating the right kind of nutrition. This content may take diverse forms, such as blog posts, podcasts, videos, social media posts, and even email newsletters.

- **Sponsorships:** Aligning your brand with a well-known athlete or another popular brand often enhances the credibility of your brand. It allows you to expand your reach while also making you stand out from your competition.

- **Retargeting:** Analyzing data from your e-commerce website can give you insights into how much the customer really wants to buy your product. For instance, if a customer added the product to their cart but didn't purchase it right away, then it suggests a high purchase intent. Retargeting these customers by mailing them reminders and using targeted advertisements is a popular promotional technique that often yields fantastic results.

- **Referral marketing:** By offering your customers incentives for referring your brand to others, you can accelerate the word-of-mouth publicity that your brand garners. This is an excellent strategy because it brings in genuine engagement, as people trust their friends to send them authentic recommendations. Offering people rewards and loyalty points may also help in building a fan following for your brand.

Financial Projections

As you can see, leveraging your NIL rights requires you to seamlessly switch between your athletic and marketing roles. However, that's not all there is to it. As an athlete-entrepreneur, you must also be well-versed in the financial side of your business. This part of your business plan encourages your investors to trust your financial acumen, thereby increasing their confidence in your business. Most athletes feel super-overwhelmed by this part of the plan, but don't worry, I've got you covered. The first thing to do is to get the financial jargon right in your mind. So, here are a few concepts that you'll encounter most frequently in your business adventure:

Income Statement vs. Balance Sheets vs. Cash Flow Statement

Before you jump into these concepts, remember that accounting is usually done in one of two ways: On a cash basis or on an accrual basis. Accrual accounting records earnings and expenses the moment they're billed, regardless of whether or not they're paid for yet, whereas cash accounting records them only after money has changed hands. This distinction proves important when we're trying to distinguish income statements, balance sheets, and cash flow statements. Without going into too many financial and accounting details, let's try to define these three and then see how they're used in making financial projections.

An income statement uses accrual accounting to assess the profitability of a business over a certain duration, such as a year, or a quarter. The idea is to deduct the cost of goods sold (COGS) from the recorded sales revenue to find gross profit. COGS refers to what it costs you to make the product including the raw materials and labor costs. However, these aren't the only costs you incur. The gross profit you've arrived at also has several other non-operating costs such as taxes or interest if you've borrowed your working capital, and operating expenses such as costs incurred to sell through particular channels, administrative costs, and so on. Once you deduct all of these expenses from your gross profits, you'll arrive at net profits which is the actual profits you're left with at the end of a specific time period. These figures may seem way too complicated at first but as you get used to them, you'll see that they're extremely effective when conveying the success of your business to a potential investor.

While the income statements determine the profitability of a business, balance sheets aim to give a full view of the assets, liabilities, and shareholders' equity at a particular time. In other words, a balance sheet at any point gives a "snapshot" of the business by outlining what the business owns, owes, and the shareholders' investment (Fernando, 2024). Balance sheets are extremely valuable to your investors because they give them crucial figures to assess the well-being of your business. For instance, they may derive the debt-to-equity (D/E) ratio from your balance sheet by comparing your liabilities with shareholder equity. Essentially, this ratio tells them how much of your business is financed with borrowed money. The higher the D/E ratio, the riskier the investment. While there's no fixed figure that you need to adhere to, you might want to ensure that your D/E ratio is comparable with your competitors. For instance, a real estate business may have a much higher D/E ratio compared to a merchandise company.

Lastly, we arrive at the cash flow statement which is a great measure of how well you manage the cash in your company. Does it generate enough cash to fulfill its debt obligations? Does it have enough to fund its operations? In essence, a cash flow statement refers to the money coming in and going out of the company. You can do this in two ways: the direct method which just lists all the receipts and payments and the indirect method which starts with the net income and then adjusts for non-cash transactions such as reductions in asset value over time referred to as depreciation.

Remember that none of these statements would give the investors a complete picture by themselves. They're generally looked at together for the most comprehensive view.

Creating Financial Projections

I know the above information sounds too technical, but here's a step-by-step financial projections guide that outlines the process in simple steps:

Step #1: Sales projection: Sales projections are usually done with either a top-down or bottom-up approach. A bottom-up approach takes into account company-specific factors such as production capacity, budgets allocated for sales and marketing, past performance, and so on. A top-down approach, on the other hand, looks at the entire market for the product along with all the competitors and makes an estimation of your potential market share. This is why serious market research is extremely critical before jumping into any business.

A bottom-up approach is relatively easy once you already have an established business with ample historical data—all you need to do is make an estimation of future sales based on past records. A top-down approach may also not be entirely accurate, and you may end up overestimating your market share. This is why the best starting point is to look at your competition and make similar assumptions for your business. Therefore, you'd need to list all the product categories with their prices, estimate the sales from your competitors, and then multiply these two figures to get the total revenue.

Step #2: Expense projection: Here, you'd consider all expenses that your business incurs and may include such things as rent, vehicles, marketing costs, wages, legal fees, and so on. While some of these may be fixed, others may fluctuate over time. This is slightly easier than sales forecasting since you're trying to predict your own expenditure choices. However, it's essential that you consider and are prepared for all factors, right from policy changes, inflation, and supply chain hurdles to even natural disasters. But how can you prepare for something so random? The idea is to keep some sort of buffer in your expense projection, maybe 10-15%, for unexpected expenses.

Step #3: Balance sheet: Once you make three divisions of assets, liabilities, and shareholder equity, it's important to remember that the asset side must always be equal to the added product of liabilities and equity; if this equation doesn't match up, there's likely an error somewhere. Here's a template for you to create your balance sheet (Indeed Editorial Team, 2023):

Assets	
1	Cash
2	Accounts receivable
3	Inventory
4	Fixed assets
5	Total assets
Liabilities	
6	Credit card debt
7	Bank loan
8	Accounts payable
9	Total liabilities

Equity	
10	Capital
11	Private or public stock amounts
12	Retained earnings
13	Total equity

Step #4: Income statement: Keeping in mind our discussion on income statements, you can go ahead and use this template by FreshBooks to create your income statement (Free income statement template, n.d.):

Revenue	Year 1	Year 2	Year 3
Sales			
Less Sales return			
Less Discounts			
Net sales			
COGS			
Material			
Labor			
Overhead			
Total COGS			

Gross Profit			
Operating expenses			
Wages			
Advertising			
Repair and maintenance			
Travel			
Rent			
Delivery/freight expense			
Utilities			
Insurance			
Mileage			
Office supplies			
Depreciation			
Interest			
Other expenses			
Total operating expenses			

Operating profit/loss			
Other income			
Interest income			
Profit/loss before taxes			
Less Tax expense			
Net profit/loss			

Step #5: Cash flow statement: Lastly, we arrive at the cash flow statement. This statement is divided into three sections: the main revenue-generating activities of your business; investing activities that bring in or use up cash; and financing activities that require you to change the equity composition of your company, such as diluting it to raise money from investors. You may find the following template useful (CFI Team, n.d.):

Operating cash flow	Year 1	Year 2	Year 3
Net earnings			
Plus Depreciation and amortization			
Less Changes in working capital			
Cash from operations			

Investing cash flow	Year 1	Year 2	Year 3
Investments in property and equipment			
Cash from investing			
Financing cash flow	Year 1	Year 2	Year 3
Repayment of debt			
Repayment of equity			
Cash from financing			
Net increase/decrease in cash			
Opening cash balance			
Closing cash balance			

With these templates, you can narrow down the most critical figures for your business plan. Again, remember that filling in these templates becomes easier with time, but the first time around, you might have to rely on some assumptions based on your competitors and the size of the size of the market.. If you've conducted high-quality market research, then the accuracy of the assumptions will also increase. I know this chapter may seem like a lot of financial and marketing jargon. However, your adventure in entrepreneurship would likely be incomplete without them. Now that you have a firm handle on the business side of things, it's time to understand what else you require to fulfill your dream of becoming a successful student-athlete entrepreneur.

Chapter 4:

The Student-Athlete Entrepreneur

In the introduction, we already touched upon the challenges that you, as a student-athlete, may face in your daily routine. However, with the arrival of the NIL laws, there's a huge addition of entrepreneurial possibilities to that student-athlete profile. You are no longer just endorsing products; you are the product, or rather the brand, yourself. While, as a college student, you're uniquely positioned to make the most of the varied career opportunities in front of you, balancing all of them isn't the easiest task. Since all three of these roles are so intertwined with one another, missing a step on one can lead to a quick downward spiral on all three fronts. Therefore, leveraging the NIL rights in the perfect manner requires that you pay attention to all of these diverse yet interconnected roles and responsibilities.

This chapter provides you with practical tips and tools to establish a balanced lifestyle that helps you reach your highest potential as a student-athlete entrepreneur. Here, we look into three crucial facets: time management, support networks, and NCAA compliance.

Time Management Strategies

A pickle jar thought experiment is a fantastic starting point for understanding the importance of time management. Here's how it goes: Take a transparent pickle jar and fill it with big pebbles. Once it's relatively full, add smaller pebbles, and then add sand till there's no more space. All of these substances are thought to be excellent metaphors for our life tasks—the big pebbles are the tasks that matter the most to you, the smaller pebbles are important but may not be at the top of your priority list, and lastly, sand encompasses the unimportant tasks that clutter your life.

Now imagine putting in the sand first. Would there be any more space for the pebbles? This is exactly what happens with many student-athlete entrepreneurs—they are so overwhelmed by the clutter of unimportant tasks that they're left with no time for things that actually matter to them. This is why it's important to fill your time with priorities first, important tasks next, and unimportant tasks last, if at all. Now, this doesn't mean that you should discard the sand altogether. Remember that recreational activities with no purpose are also important for you to recharge, but it's all about filling the jar in the right order.

Time management may seem like a cliche phrase that everyone, including your teachers, parents, sponsors, and coaches, throws at you thanks to your multifaceted lifestyle. The problem is, though, that no one really tells you *how* you can actually manage your time better. That's exactly what we're going to tackle in this session.

Before we start, however, I want you to remember that time management isn't a foreign concept to you. If you are a student-athlete aspiring to be an entrepreneur, you're already juggling quite a few things, and that's no easy feat. Now, we shall try to streamline those efforts by using specific practical techniques that are easy to implement.

SMART Goal-Setting

No time management techniques can help unless you have a clear vision of your own goals. What exactly are you managing time for? That's the first question you need to ask, and the answer to that is one of the most foundational time management strategies. Of course, this on its own doesn't tell you how to manage time, but it gives you the framework on which to base other strategies that we'll discuss in a while. For now, it's important that you define your goals as specifically as possible.

SMART is an apt acronym for a five-criteria framework that includes specific, measurable, achievable, relevant, and time-bound.

Here are a few questions that you can answer to narrow down your goals, regardless of whether they are in academics, athletics, or business:

Specific	What do I want to accomplish? What are the details? What resources are available to me? Are there any other stakeholders involved in this?
Measurable	How do I plan to measure the progress? How do I quantify it?
Achievable	Are you equipped with the right skills and capabilities? Are you sure you can achieve this?
Relevant	Why this particular goal? Why is it important to me?
Time-bound	By when do I want to achieve this goal? What's the timeline that I want to assign to this goal?

Pareto Principle

Pareto analysis, also known as the 80/20 rule, says that 80% of the outputs come from only 20% of the inputs. The Pareto principle is often referred to as the "universal truth" (Kruse, 2016). This is because it applies to several aspects of life: time management, business revenue, academics, and so on. 20% of the product categories often bring 80% of the revenue; 20% of the study material will often contain key concepts that cover 80% of the tests; and most importantly, 20% of your tasks can fulfill 80% of your goals. The trick is to identify the right 20% to get to the 80%.

Now, understand that the Pareto principle comes with certain caveats. Firstly, the 80/20 ratio is an approximation and may change depending on the situation. Secondly, it doesn't suggest that you only expend 20% of the effort. Interestingly, the Pareto principle doesn't talk about efforts at all. It talks about 80% of outcomes resulting from 20% of causes. So, the question isn't about how much effort you expend but rather about whether that effort is channeled in the right direction. Lastly, remember that the 20% of causes may get you to the 80% mark in your goals, but the journey from 80 to 100 will probably take up a lot more effort. That being said, it's valuable in time management solely because it helps you identify those 20% of the actions that can supercharge your progress as a student-athlete entrepreneur. It can help you set the right priorities so that you can get more things done without necessarily spending excessive time on them. So here's how the implementation of this strategy would go:

1. Identify the most critical tasks that will help you achieve the maximum number of goals.

2. Try to figure out the challenges and their root causes that you face on your path to goal fulfillment.

3. Assign a score to each of these causes.

4. Prioritize working on the causes with the highest score; that's your 20%.

Eisenhower Matrix

A very real problem that you, as a student-athlete entrepreneur, are likely to face is the overwhelming number of tasks on your plate. I bet you wish you had a system that would tell you which tasks are worth your time and which ones aren't. The Eisenhower Matrix does exactly that. It's a framework that divides your tasks into four quadrants based on their importance and urgency. Take a look:

	Urgent	**Not Urgent**
Important	**Do:** These are both important and urgent tasks that need to be completed within a given timeframe.	**Decide:** These are important but not urgent. Ex: Spending time with loved ones;

	Ex: Preparing for an upcoming test or game; making the delivery deadlines in your business; addressing unexpected emergencies as an entrepreneur.	planning for future business expansion; proactive social media strategy planning.
Not Important	**Delegate:** These are urgent tasks but add no value. Ex: Answering certain emails, phone calls, or errands.	**Delete:** These tasks are neither important nor urgent. Ex: Time spent watching TV; busy work such as meetings without definite agendas.

Time-Blocking

Do you ever look at some extremely busy people and wonder how they do it? It's almost as if they have extra hours in the day that the rest of us don't. In reality, however, they are just better at managing their time. If you struggle to understand how they do this, then you might find the time-blocking strategy particularly useful. Here, you'll divide the day into time blocks, with each block assigned to a particular time.

6.00 a.m. to 7.30 a.m.	Training
8.00 a.m. to 11.00 a.m.	Class
11.30 a.m. to 1.00 p.m.	Business proposal

1.30 p.m. to 2.30 p.m.	Social media posting
2.30 p.m. to 5.30 p.m.	Class
6.00 p.m. to 8.00 p.m.	Socializing with loved ones
8.30 p.m. to 10.00 p.m.	Test preparation

Ensure that you keep time buffers in between your tasks to account for unexpected situations and keep yourself from being overwhelmed.

Pomodoro Technique

There is a concept known as Parkinson's Law that states that work expands to fill the time assigned to it. In other words, if you assign an hour to complete an essay, it will be done within an hour; if you give it a day, you may find that you require the entire day to finish it. Now, this isn't a time management technique in itself, but it can be used quite effectively in combination with something known as the Pomodoro technique. This technique tries to enhance your productivity by breaking the work down into short spurts. This technique is fantastic when you feel burnt out. This is how it works:

1. Work on one specific task for a specific period of time, let's say, 25 minutes. Set the timer for the same.

2. When the timer goes off, take a break for about two to five minutes. Do something that's unrelated to the work you were doing.

3. After the break, repeat step one. Once you've done this four times, you can take longer breaks of 20–30 minutes.

So, if you can use the "Pomodoros" to break your work into smaller tasks as per Parkinson's Law, you keep the tasks tight while also sticking to a timeline.

All of these techniques can either be used individually or in combination with each other. Just make sure that you ease into it rather than taking on everything all at once. While overwhelming yourself is one end of the spectrum, procrastination is the other. How often do you tell yourself you'll start tomorrow, especially when things are a little outside your comfort zone? If you are a procrastinator too, then Brian Tracy has wonderful advice for you.

Mark Twain once said, "If it's your job to eat a frog, it's best to do it first thing in the morning. And If it's your job to eat two frogs, it's best to eat the biggest one first." (Twain, n.d.) In his book *Eat That Frog* (2017), Tracy draws from this wisdom and suggests that you tackle those tasks first that, you are most likely to procrastinate. So, if you're likely to put off the social media data analysis for later because you aren't fond of numbers, you might want to tackle that first thing in the day. When you combine this understanding with the above techniques, you're bound to see fantastic improvements in your time management skills.

Building a Social Support Network

One thing sports teach you is that no matter what game you play, how efficient you are, or how skilled and talented you are, you still need your team to win, even in individual sports. Being a successful student-athlete entrepreneur requires not only honed business acumen but also the ability to leverage your network. Now, leveraging your network doesn't mean you go about handing out your business cards in the hope of making the right business connections. When I talk about your network, I mean the ability to nurture genuine relationships.

Believe it or not, your social support network is one of the most valuable assets on your path to entrepreneurship. A strong social circle comes with tremendous benefits, and it's not just about feeling good when you're with your loved ones. Not only do they provide you with emotional support, they also offer physical help and informational support in the form of advice, guidance, and mentoring. When your days are brimming over with academic, athletic, and entrepreneurial responsibilities, having the right kind of people to lean on is critical.

Here are a few people you might want to have in your corner, apart from your friends and family:

- **Academic advisors:** These professionals may have several different designations, such as athletic academic specialists and coordinators of athletic academic services. Whatever the name, their job is to oversee the academic performance of student-athletes. In other words, they ensure that you and your team maintain the NCAA's Academic Progress Rate without which you run the risk of losing scholarships, facing practice time and membership restrictions, and so on. These advisors often help with tasks such as

    o course registration

    o scheduling and monitoring class attendance

    o coordinating tutoring and mentoring sessions for student-athletes who need more support

    o post-graduation career guidance

- **Athletic coaches and trainers:** This is an obvious one since student-athletes spend so much time with coaches and trainers. However, they both perform distinct functions. While a coach's main goal is to leverage your athletic skills to enhance the team's performance, a trainer is more focused on improving your athletic performance as an individual athlete. A coach has several responsibilities, such as

    o injury prevention

    o nutrition

    o risk management with evaluation of facilities and equipment

- o An athletic trainer, on the other hand, is more concerned with

- o skill development and mastery

- o recovery and rehabilitation

- o inculcating resilience and other mental skills into physical training

- o Even though their functions are different, their goal must be the same: improving your performance.

- **Time management coaches:** No mystery in what these professionals do—they help you manage time as you juggle all your diverse responsibilities. It may seem like you can do it on your own, but remember that there's no shame in asking for help. A time management coach would help you

  - o improve focus and productivity

  - o goal-setting and achievement

  - o improve planning skills

  - o prioritize what really matters

  - o While any time management coach would help, you might want to look for someone who has experience working with student-athlete entrepreneurs.

- **Business advisors:** Entrepreneurship in itself is a challenging role, and doing it in addition to your student-athlete responsibilities means that the odds are probably going to be stacked against you. Having a reliable business advisor who is aligned with your long-term vision can be a terrific asset. Business advisors perform varied duties, such as

  - o recommending the best possible business strategy

- o preparing budgets for the company and assessing the financial records to ensure that you are on the right track

  - o identifying business expansion opportunities

  - o advising on the marketing and sales strategy based on consumer behavior research

- **Financial advisors:** While these professionals may offer advice on your business finances, their main focus tends to be your personal finances. The money that you make through your business must be channeled in the right manner to reap the full benefits of your business. Therefore, a financial advisor may help you with long-term wealth planning with

  - o investments

  - o tax planning

  - o retirement planning

  - o debt management

  - o insurance planning

- **Legal counsel:** Since compliance considerations are at the core of your student-athlete entrepreneur career, having trusted legal counsel is a must. These legal professionals can help you

  - o identify NIL opportunities

  - o draft the right licensing agreements

  - o negotiate beneficial NIL deals

  - o recognize conflicts between new and existing NIL deals

Remember that building a network isn't a contest of getting all the above professionals for your collection. It takes a lot more to build a genuine support network.

Building Strong Relationships

Sure, the kind of professionals you have in your network is extremely important, but an even more important question is this: Would these professionals come to your aid when you need them? This is where the relationships that you nurture with those in your network become crucial. Finding the right people is one thing, and ensuring that they stay with you on your journey is another. Therefore, building a strong social support network demands that you make a conscious effort to lay a strong foundation for your relationships. Here are a few communication tips to consider:

1. **Goal assessment:** Only when you're clear about the kind of support you're looking for will you be able to find it. For instance, if you're looking to meet other athlete entrepreneurs, you're less likely to find them by joining, let's say, a cooking class. Knowing what kind of people you're looking to meet will dictate the like-minded communities that you can join.

2. **Active listening:** At the core of any meaningful relationship is the ability to listen. Sure, it may be tempting to get down to business right away, but if you're looking to form long-lasting relationships, then you must listen to their story as much as you tell them yours. Show them that you're genuinely interested in what they tell you, both with your words and with your body language.

3. **Support:** An excellent way to build a strong network is to offer support whenever possible. Let's say a fellow athlete is seeking some legal advice, and you think your legal counsel could help. All it takes is two minutes to connect them, and you've instantly cemented a great relationship with both the athlete and the lawyer.

4. **Boundary-setting:** As important as offering support is, it's also important to recognize when you aren't in a position to do it. Boundaries are a critical component of strong relationships. Being assertive and saying "no" and also respecting others' right

to say "no" ensures that the mental well-being of everyone involved is prioritized.

Navigating NCAA Compliance

The National Collegiate Athletic Association (NCAA) is the governing body that sets the rules and regulations that college athletes must abide by. The big-picture idea is to maintain intercollegiate sports as an integral part of the student-athlete's educational experience. While your legal counsel is certainly an expert on these regulations, it's crucial that you understand the basics of the NCAA policies to avoid getting into sticky spots. Before diving into these policies, however, note that this book and this section are for informational purposes only; for the latest information, you must consult with your university compliance officers.

The NCAA has certain basic eligibility criteria that you must fulfill. Let's do a quick run-through of these:

1. **Academic requirements:** As much as the NCAA is about sports, it's also about academics. As a student-athlete, you're expected to submit rigorous eligibility criteria.

    A. **High school coursework:** The NCAA requires you to complete a specific set of high school courses to be eligible. The exact requirements tend to vary depending on the division that you're playing in.

    B. **Grade point average:** You must have a minimum GPA in your coursework.

    C. **Standardized test scores:** You'd need to submit your scores on standardized tests such as the SAT and ACT to the NCAA Eligibility Center.

2. **Ethical conduct requirements:** The NCAA has very specific policies regarding gambling, drug use, and unsportsmanlike

conduct, which, if not abided by, can result in disciplinary sanctions ranging from suspension to permanent ineligibility.

3. **The NIL rule:** This is, of course, the core of our discussion. While we may not be able to dig into the intricate details of the NIL rules here, you need to know that NIL rules tend to vary based on the state you're located in and your college. If the state where you attend college doesn't enforce any NIL laws, you can still profit from NIL activities, and there's no limit on how much you can earn from these activities. That being said, you might want to be mindful of how your earnings may impact your financial aid eligibility.

Since the NIL landscape is governed primarily by state laws, gauging your NIL rights can be a confusing task. However, it's still crucial that you figure them out accurately because without knowing them, you run the risk of losing your eligibility. Moreover, these rules and regulations are constantly changing, and that's why you need to stay on top of these changes. If you aren't sure of these, then you may even consider professional service providers to help you leverage the NIL rules in the best possible manner. Be aware, however, that the NCAA still does not allow you to use marketing agents to advertise yourself to play for a professional team.

Speaking of what the NIL laws don't allow for, here are a few things your NIL rights prohibit (AWM Capital, 2022):

- Performance-based incentives.

- NIL compensation from your school or college

- Compensation for athletic participation or achievement.

- Endorsement of certain categories of goods (alcohol, casinos, tobacco, etc.)

- Use of school logos in their endorsements unless the school specifies otherwise

- NIL compensation to attend a specific school

While these basics are a great starting point, they cannot replace the valuable compliance resources provided by the NCAA and your university. The NCAA compliance webpage is a great reference for anyone who wishes to understand the latest policies. Also, be sure to check out your university website or even visit them personally to inquire about the NIL rules. Additionally, you may want to check out the following resources:

A. **Websites:**

1.   eligibilitycenter.org for registration and documentation details

2.   https://www.ncaa.org/sports/2021/2/8/about-taking-action.aspx for the latest information on NCAA policies

3.   on.ncaa.com/IntlContact for international student eligibility

B. **Hotlines**

1.   317-223-0706 for NIL questions

2.   317-917-6222 for general NCAA questions

Building a Compliant Business Model

Understand that the NIL rules are still fairly new and that student-athlete entrepreneurs are still finding their way around to establish NIL-compliant business models. Also, remember that no matter what business you're aiming for, it'll be under the scrutiny of both NIL laws and other relevant laws that guide any other company in that state. For instance, when endorsing a product, in addition to the NIL requirements for disclosures and licenses, you may also need to be aware of the Federal Trade Commission guides, which regulate the disclosures that must be included in any sponsored social media posts of product endorsements. If you're leveraging the NIL rights in the form of NFTs, you must have a strong grasp of securities and tax regulations.

Now, this in-depth understanding will be very specific to your industry and sub-industry. However, there are a few other points that may be applicable to you regardless of the business you choose. Let's focus on some key points that you need to keep in mind when starting your own venture:

- **Intellectual property:** I mentioned this in the first chapter, but it's worth repeating again: You must ensure that your logo or business name isn't infringing on another company's intellectual property. Do a basic Google search before you finalize the branding information. If you have a unique product that your company offers, then you may also want to check out the U.S. Patent and Trademark Office's (USPTO) Trademark Electronic Search System (TESS) before filing for a patent. Taking these measures ensures that you can protect your own brand from any future infringement by sending a cease-and-desist letter or even filing an infringement lawsuit.

- **Business registration:** While you don't necessarily need to form an LLC to profit from NIL, in most cases, it's actually a great idea. This is especially true once you start making larger amounts of money, as LLC registration helps you compartmentalize your personal and business income and also reduces your personal liability. So, even though it requires an upfront investment of a couple hundred bucks (this varies from state to state), it does offer great benefits in the long run.

- **Contracts and agreements:** If you're working with an agency, make sure you have an air-tight representation contract with them. These usually include the enlisted services, payment terms, terms of contract renewal and termination, and required disclosures. This level of detail applies not only to the agency contracts but also to your NIL deals and any other transactions that you conduct with other parties.

As I mentioned before, navigating NIL compliance becomes much easier with the right legal experts, and you should definitely consider onboarding them. Now that you have a detailed understanding of what it takes to be a NIL entrepreneur, it's time to get a true view of the success that NIL can bring to your career.

Chapter 5:

Athlete Success Stories

Knowing what you now know about NIL rights, becoming an entrepreneur, and the technicalities of actually starting a business, you might be tempted to wonder: *How on earth am I going to do all that?!* If that question crosses your mind, then don't worry; you aren't the only one. Very few sports personalities get into the field to become entrepreneurs; they get in for the love of the sport, their passion, and pure hard work. However, it cannot be denied that the world of sports provides endless entrepreneurial opportunities for young athletes all over, especially with the introduction of the NIL rules. Even though business may not have been your goal initially, ignoring these opportunities would be a massive disservice to your love of sports.

All said and done, the entrepreneurial journey of a student-athlete is also ridden with hurdles and challenges. We all know of big names in sports that have seamlessly transitioned into entrepreneurship, such as Steph Curry, LeBron James, Serena Williams, Tiger Woods, and the list goes on. However, not all of us are aware of student-athletes who have gone on to make their mark in the business world. This chapter focuses on a few success stories that will undoubtedly inspire you to go on this adventure of self-discovery by yourself.

Student-Athlete Entrepreneur Success Stories

Student-athletes are often faced with the brutal choice between transforming their athletic skills and experience into a full-fledged career or taking on another profession altogether. Even though a career in sports is all you aspire to, the unfortunate truth of the matter is that a very small percentage of student-athletes actually go on to become professional athletes. If statistical figures are to be believed, only 1.6%

of college football players go on to play in the NFL (Schultz, 2024). Of course, you can be sure that the competitive, disciplined, athletic side of your personality will have your back no matter what your choice is. But the point is that you, as a student-athlete, will need to focus on being financially independent at some point, and the NIL rights give you the perfect opportunity to transition into a self-sufficient entrepreneur. Take a look at the following three student-athletes who built a meaningful and profitable business.

#1 The Southern Comfort Kitchen Story

William Matthews from New Orleans received the Kent State University athletics scholarship and moved more than a thousand miles away to finish his education (From running back to entrepreneur, 2024). Will did exceptionally well as a running back for the Golden Flashes and even scored a touchdown to take his team to the first-ever bowl game victory in program history. However, that's not all that Will excelled at—he turned out to be as good with the ladle as he was with the ball.

When he moved to Kent, Ohio, he realized there was a distinct change in his environment. He missed his family and the Cajun flavors they cooked up. So, he would call back home and ask for recipes for his favorites, such as jambalaya, bread pudding, and gumbo. He began by cooking for himself and his friends. He figured pretty soon that he was good at it and decided to give entrepreneurship a real shot.

Being an entrepreneurship major, he knew that a good business plan was at the core of the success of his idea. So, in his junior year, he created a 32-page business plan for a New Orleans-themed restaurant for his New Venture Creations class. For this presentation, he brought in a few samples that he had cooked, and one of his classmates, Zack Mottershead, was immensely impressed with the flavors. The two then joined hands and started looking to raise funds to get this business going. They got their boost when they entered a business pitch competition in their senior year and won second place, which fetched them $1,000, which they eventually used to buy equipment and their food truck.

Aptly named, the Southern Comfort Kitchen, Will and Mark's food truck, remains open from March to November, and when the weather gets too harsh, they cater events such as parties, office lunches, concerts, and weddings. They have a strong online community of over 6,000 Instagram and 4,000 Facebook followers, which they use to post the truck's main hours. Their business has enjoyed great success since they started and seems to always have a queue of people waiting for their orders. They have also opened a brick-and-mortar restaurant in Akron, Ohio.

While Will credits the entrepreneurship program at Kent University, his grit cannot be overstated. In an interview, he was quoted saying, "I appreciate Ohio for not having the best food because it gave me the thought process to move forward with this business." (Schreck, 2022) This ability to see opportunity in adversity is an absolute must for anyone willing to walk in Will's footsteps.

#2 Building The Motus Studios

In 2023, Malik Pottinger, a former Varsity Blues student-athlete on the men's basketball team, made history with his sister, Sydnie Pottinger, also a former Varsity student-athlete on the women's volleyball team. With their clothing brand, The Motus Studios, they became the first students to partner with the University of Toronto's Trademark Licensing program (Sibling start-up, 2024).

The conception of The Motus Studios began around the pandemic. During this time, the two siblings started exploring the clothing that checked the stylish yet comfortable box and found that there was a real gap between the options available and the demand. This is when they decided to get down and dirty as entrepreneurs. Not only did they design the clothing line, but they also took on the responsibility of manufacturing and shipping the items to their customers. As if this wasn't enough, they even designed their own logo and created a brand from scratch.

As they saw that their brand and products were being worn and recognized, they realized that it was time to take the next step toward a brick-and-mortar store. Being students of the University of Toronto, their first obvious choice for physical presence was their university's bookstore. Sydnie Pottinger recalls being hesitant about approaching the university's licensing office when her parents encouraged them by reminding them of a simple detail: "The worst that can happen is that the bookstore says no." (Sibling start-up, 2024).

This turned out to be fantastic advice, as approaching the university not only allowed them to leverage the university logo but also put them in touch with the program manager, Ivan Canete. Canete had been working with the famous "Under Armor" brand, and his experience in marketing proved to be a great asset in the collaboration between the Pottingers and the university. The university partnership was pivotal as it stocked the brand's items in its bookstore, invested in the initial inventory, and even connected them to crucial resources such as the Black Entrepreneurs Network.

Malik remarks about the fitting nature of their brand name: "MOTUS is Latin for motion, and it fits us as we always have one foot ahead, and it signifies always progressing and elevating." He confesses to having faced several challenges, such as making the brand work while he is in school or the lack of experience in terms of what really goes into branding and selling the product. However, the Pottingers have been able to tap into their most valuable resource, which is their family network. Malik explains how their roles are clearly defined: Sydnie takes on product development, he focuses on business structure and operations, and their younger sister Callie oversees marketing.

After the brilliant initial success where the company sold out 90% of its inventory in the first 72 hours, Malik plans to spend his first year after graduation building the business. He already has well-defined goals, such as the production of leather goods, which allows the company to channel its efforts in the most lucrative direction.

#3 "Inkspiring" Athletes All over

Inquoris "Inky" Johnson was always athletically gifted. Coming from humble beginnings, he aspired to be an NFL player to overcome the hard-hitting financial challenges he had seen growing up. This dream was about to be fulfilled when his hard work landed him in the top

0.00057% percentile of college athletes in his competing year (Palmeri, 2023). His excellent statistics as a star cornerback for the Tennessee Volunteers meant that he would be a projected top-30 NFL draft pick. Everything was going to plan when Inky was about to realize that life had other plans for him.

In 2006, Inky suffered a life-changing injury on the field and woke up after an emergency surgery with a paralyzed right arm. As expected, the 2006 draft pick didn't include him, and he had to make peace with the distressing realization that the sports career that he had worked so hard for was now over.

At this point, Inky could have easily stayed down, and no one could fault him for it. But his grit pulled him out of rock bottom and was instrumental in establishing a new career from scratch. Though athletics was no longer on the cards, he went back to college and graduated with a sports psychology degree. Today, he's a renowned motivational speaker and the founder of Inkspire LLC. He has a whopping 693,000 Instagram followers and an estimated net worth of over a million dollars (Cardoso, 2022).

Lessons Learned

The above three success stories are diverse in their own way. Be it the type of business that these entrepreneurs built or the circumstances that led to their entrepreneurship. Even though these may seem like cheesy inspirational stories that often do the rounds on social media, there's much to learn from these instances. Consider the following lessons that these success stories teach us about entrepreneurship:

- **Opportunity identification:** Where regular folks see problems, entrepreneurs perceive opportunities. Apart from Inkspire, which we shall talk about in just a while, the two other businesses did a fantastic job identifying existing market opportunities. When you analyze their business path, you'll quickly notice that they follow Harvard professor, Clayton Christensen's disruptive theory very well.

Christensen suggests that there are two kinds of market disruptions: low-end market opportunities and new market opportunities (Cote, 2022). Low-end disruption occurs when new businesses claim the lower market segments with the bare minimum profits. This means that those companies with higher market shares may not really care to fight back. However, over time, the new entrant keeps moving upward, capturing higher profitability segments. Take the case of the Southern Comfort Kitchen: They began their journey as a small food truck and have only now expanded to a full-fledged restaurant.

The other type of market disruption is new market opportunities, which are focused on creating a new market segment altogether. Here, the new company realizes that the market is saturated with the current range of products and that customers are looking for something new. The Motus Studios, for instance, identified that their target demographic was looking for something stylish but comfortable. This opportunity identification eventually led them to create designs that resonated with their market.

Inkspire LLC, as a business, may not fit into the disruption category, but it teaches you the value of a growth mindset in your business journey. A person with a growth mindset is aware that in-born talent is only a small factor in life success. When Inky was prevented from using his athletic gifts, he knew that he had to dig deeper and uncover exceptional grit to move forward. He not only flipped adversity on its head but utilized that tragedy to create something much bigger that brought both meaning and financial success into his life.

- **Branding strategy:** We've already discussed the process of strategizing your brand in detail, but it's worth taking a moment to see how these companies capitalized on their respective brands while building a successful business. For instance, the Southern Comfort Kitchen may not have been as popular if he hadn't branded it around Cajun flavors; the Motus Studios may not have garnered the attention of their university demographic if the Pottingers hadn't centered their brand around stylish comfort for young people; and Inkspire may not have reached thousands if Inky hadn't built a motivational brand around his own story. It was because of this specific niche branding that these businesses found their unique voice.

However, it wasn't only about the stories that these brands chose to tell. Rather, all of these entrepreneurs were extremely skilled at utilizing the available resources to the fullest. The Motus Studios made the perfect move to leverage their University of Toronto connection; Matthews of Southern Comfort Kitchen made the right decision to join hands with Mottershead; and Inky found a way to turn his deepest misfortune into a profitable brand.

- **Balancing athletics and entrepreneurship:** By now, you have a clear understanding of the challenges you're likely to face on your student-athlete entrepreneurship path. The idea is not to scare you but to ensure that you're prepared to take on these challenges in the best possible manner. This is where the above businesses offer great insights. Of course, time management was a necessary skill, but here are a few more practical tips that these businesses employed:

  o **Delegation:** No one can do it all on their own; it's important to lean on your close circle of people. Take, for instance, The Motus Studios: Their success would probably be impossible if Malik or Sydnie had been adamant about doing it individually. They were able to recognize their academic, athletic, and entrepreneurial roles and responsibilities and divide the tasks based on individual strengths.

  o **Realistic goals:** Dreaming big is great, but when it comes to your goals, it's better to keep them just outside your reach. Southern Comfort Kitchen knew that the first step to success was allowing their food to connect with people on a personal level rather than investing in a full-fledged restaurant setup, and their food truck helped them lay the perfect foundation to build a loyal customer base.

o **Self-care:** Taking time out for yourself is a critical part of balancing skills that are often overlooked. When Inky was given the negative verdict by the doctors, he focused on recovering to the best possible extent and went back to his education. This focus on himself gave him the time to process his loss and also come up with a creative business idea. Even when downtime seems like time wasted, it gives you a different perspective and may help you come back from adversity even stronger.

Though we haven't explicitly focused on the ups and downs that these student-athlete entrepreneurs may have faced, you can be sure that it wasn't a smooth-sailing journey for any of them. Entrepreneurship isn't about the opportunities that are handed to you but about what you make of those opportunities, even in the face of adversity. Apart from all these lessons, one key lesson to remember is that no matter how well you plan and strategize, you'll face unexpected challenges. There's no set formula for overcoming them, but the process of working through them will itself teach you a lot more than any book ever can. The important thing to remember is that you aren't alone. You have an entire ecosystem to fall back on. In the next chapter, we evaluate the role of universities, which are a critical part of that ecosystem.

Chapter 6:

The Role of Universities

Till this point, we've focused only on how NIL impacts student-athletes. Sure, they're the heroes of this adventure, but the universities that these student-athletes represent also have a pivotal supporting role to play. It's also worth noting that the implementation of the NIL rules means big bucks not just for the concerned athletes but also for the colleges and universities in which they study. This means that these educational institutions have their funds and reputation at stake, which is more than enough boost to play an active role in the NIL entrepreneurial journey of their students.

The involvement of universities is generally two-fold: The courses they offer that promote entrepreneurship among their student-athletes and the NIL guidance and compliance resources. This chapter gives you an insight into both of these aspects so that you can fully tap into the benefits that your university program offers.

Guidance and Compliance

Earlier, we saw the NCAA's NIL policies that student-athletes must be mindful of. While many NIL violations went scot-free in the initial period after the introduction of NIL laws, the NCAA is now much more stringent about the enforcement of these laws. The universities tend to play a critical role in this enforcement and are given the responsibility of following the NIL rules and monitoring their continued compliance with them. Let's take a look at the specific NIL restrictions that universities must familiarize themselves with.

Infractions and Enforcement of the NCAA Regulations

The NCAA is a massive organization made up of over a thousand colleges, which means that it relies on these institutions to enforce the rules and regulations that the central body comes up with. These rules are usually extremely elaborate, such as those that regulate when and how often coaches may communicate with prospective student-athletes, or even take their incoming calls. Universities have an Enforcement Staff that ensures that such rules are abided by. If this group of employees finds that certain rules aren't being followed, it may allege either Level I or Level II violations, with Level I being more serious. These violations are then brought to the Committee on Infractions (COI), which then determines the validity of these allegations.

These infractions may be resolved in three different ways (Lens, 2023):

- **Negotiated resolution:** Here, both parties agree on the facts, violations, and penalties.

- **Summary disposition:** Here, both parties are on the same page regarding the facts and violations but not about the penalties.

- **Hearing:** This is very similar to a court hearing where the university, the individuals, and a COI panel determine the validity of the allegations made by the Enforcement Staff and then impose the penalties that the panel deems fit. The penalties may range from monetary fines to scholarship reductions and postseason bans.

You must know that if an individual is found guilty, the university is also held accountable by the NCAA.

Note that the above process applies to violations of all NCAA regulations, including the NIL rules. However, NIL compliance can be trickier than the other rules because the interim NIL policy of 2021, which permits the monetization of athletes' NIL, is pretty basic in nature. Sure, the NCAA has provided multiple clarifications since then, but the understanding of these rules still remains murky. For instance, the interim policy prohibited compensation that was (Lynam & Smith, 2024):

- contingent upon enrollment at a particular institution;

- solely for athletic participation (i.e., "pay-for-play");

- paid for no services in return (i.e., gifted and not a part of a "quid pro quo" transaction); and

- directly from the institution in exchange for the use of a student athlete's NIL.

This means that student-athletes can now earn money directly through promotions and sponsorships and through the NIL collectives, which we shall discuss in detail in the next chapter. However, even though collectives aren't prohibited, they're still a topic of quite a bit of debate as some universities are found to get student-athletes to pick their school through profitable NIL deals, which the NCAA explicitly forbids.

It is this uncertainty within the NCAA rules that makes monitoring NIL rules a daunting task for universities. This is why they may subject you to strict and often tiresome scrutiny criteria, such as reviewing your NIL agreements and forms, and even holding individual annual meetings to inquire about your NIL arrangements.

Compliance Resources to Look for

Though the NCAA is the apex governing body, remember that your school sets its own NIL policies in addition to the NCAA regulations. These policies may be aimed at protecting the school's intellectual property, such as its logo or its reputation, by association, which may prevent you from endorsing substances such as alcohol and tobacco. Since these policies may be quite elaborate in themselves, the universities are obligated to provide you with the relevant resources.

This can take several forms, which are also governed by the NCAA directives:

- **Dedicated NIL resources:** Many universities have established dedicated NIL departments to assist their student-athletes on their entrepreneurial journeys. Of course, these departments must meet strict standards of scrutiny, such as refraining from marketing their student-athletes' athletic abilities to agents, upholding state and federal legislation, monitoring the collective, and reporting any violations to the NCAA. The Ohio State University's Edge Team is a great example of the NIL resource movement. This team not only helps student-athletes tap into their maximum NIL potential but also works with companies to facilitate NIL opportunities. The OSU also has a dedicated page, NIL Simplified, that allows companies to fill out a form to indicate the players they'd like to work with and leave their contact information. OSU also implements the Corporate Ambassador Program, through which student-athletes can receive marketing training and experience while promoting several company brands (Nsouli and King, 2022). Therefore, when choosing your university, it's highly recommended that you look for one that nurtures your athletic entrepreneurship experience with as many of these dedicated resources as possible.

- **Educational resources:** Apart from the NIL resources, universities also offer educational resources that help student-athletes navigate their finances while staying compliant with NIL rules. These may include financial literacy programs on topics such as budgeting, credit score maintenance, investment planning, and so on. The athletic departments and entrepreneurship programs may also conduct seminars and workshops on ethical business practices such as contract understanding, intellectual property rights, avoiding conflicts of interest, and responsible advertising.

- **Advocacy support:** Universities are uniquely positioned to advocate on behalf of their student-athletes by helping the student-athletes fully capitalize on their NIL negotiations without compromising their financial well-being. Note that the universities still aren't allowed to directly compensate these athletes for their NIL as per the NCAA guidelines. However, the updated proposals of January 2024 (which are likely to go into effect in August 2024) allow universities to "identify potential NIL opportunities... and even facilitate deals between student-athletes and third parties." (Conniff *et al.*, 2024). For instance, your school may be able to offer you great insights on fair NIL compensation for endorsements and may even be able to negotiate on your behalf.

Finding the Perfect Program

As you can see, your choice of university can have quite an impact on your ability to leverage the NIL rules in your favor. As a student-athlete, going to an NCAA school must definitely be a top priority. NCAA schools offer you unmatched exposure to academic, athletic, financial, and networking resources. Not only do you get to compete with the most elite student-athletes, but you can also go on enlightening journeys of personal growth. However, choosing the right institution for you can be an overwhelming task. You may want to keep these three broad guidelines in mind so that you can choose the perfect program for you:

- **Check for the best college athletic programs:** The NCAA has over a thousand universities, and choosing among these requires that you look at the top contenders very carefully. The sports that you play will be an important consideration. Here are the top 10 college athletic programs that you might want to look at (Hough, 2024):

    o The **University of Florida** offers great programs for college football, women's tennis, men's golf, and women's gymnastics.

    o The **University of North Carolina at Chapel Hill** has a rich basketball legacy.

o The **University of Alabama** has a fantastic history with football, men's golf, and women's gymnastics.

o The **University of Notre Dame** does excellent in football, women's soccer, and fencing.

o **Stanford University** is known for its baseball, soccer, and tennis programs.

o The **University of Texas at Austin** has numerous sports programs, including football, baseball, swimming, track and field, and volleyball.

o **Louisiana State University** offers great track and field and baseball programs.

o The **University of Southern California** is renowned for its programs in football, tennis, water polo, golf, basketball, swimming, volleyball, and soccer.

o **Ohio State University** has been home to athletes who have won over 100 Olympic medals and also won national championships in football, baseball, and men's basketball.

o The **University of Oklahoma** has a long-standing history of success in football, wrestling, and gymnastics.

- **Leverage your courses:** The academic courses you take aren't just a means to get a college degree; they can bring valuable practical insights for your entrepreneurial journey. You may find your university offers courses in entrepreneurship, business management, marketing, or topics specifically related to NIL and athlete branding. You want to look for courses that allow you to apply theoretical lessons to bring your own business idea to life. Many universities offer business simulation projects or entrepreneurship competitions where they can test their skills, gain valuable feedback, network with like-minded people, and even make necessary adjustments to their initial plans.

- **Look for business development programs:** If you remember the Southern Comfort Kitchen story from the last chapter, you'll remember how Matthews and Mottershead benefited from the entrepreneurship program at Kent University. Here are a few entrepreneurship resources that you need to look for:

  - **Business Development Workshops:** Look for workshops offered by the entrepreneurship centers at the universities. These workshops may cover topics such as developing business plans, securing funding, and marketing strategies relevant to athlete-entrepreneurs.

  - **Mentorship Programs:** Many universities offer mentorship programs that connect students with experienced business professionals. Inquire with the athletic department or career center about the available mentorship opportunities specifically for student-athlete entrepreneurs.

  - **Business Incubators:** Some universities have business incubators that provide resources, workspace, and potential funding opportunities for student-owned ventures. You want to check your university's offerings in this arena and see if your business qualifies.

- Understanding the role that your university plays in maximizing your entrepreneurial potential is crucial if you want to make the most of the available opportunities. However, it's also important to know that your university is only one piece of the puzzle, with the NIL collectives being the other critical piece, which we shall talk about in the next chapter.

Chapter 7:

The Rise of NIL Collectives

Considering that NIL is an ecosystem with big bucks, universities can't be the only ones holding down the fort. With the arrival of NIL rules that allowed student-athletes to benefit from sponsorships and endorsements, the next obvious question was how they would connect to these opportunities. This is where the NIL collectives come in. These collectives can be quite complex, and you, as a student-athlete entrepreneur, must have the best possible understanding of how they work. This chapter attempts to give you a strategic, ethical, and legal view of the NIL collectives.

Workings of the NIL Collectives

NIL collectives operate with the aim of raising money for athletes' potential NIL opportunities. They're often created by influential alumni and supporters of the university teams. The NIL collective money comes from three sources: a commercial branding relationship with businesses, small donors who shell out a few bucks as a subscription fee on a monthly basis, and lastly, the much bigger donors who cough up thousands of dollars. Though it's not at all mandatory for universities to have their own collectives, their absence may mean that the university and its student-athletes are left behind in the ultra-competitive market of branding and recruiting. There are a few different types of collectives:

- **The donor collective:** This is the most common type of collective where funds are pooled from several members, and that pool is then used to pay athletes for NIL-compliant activities such as appearances, endorsements, social media posts, and so on. Before these collectives came in, it wasn't uncommon for rich donors, also known as boosters, to swoop in and offer money to the athletes under the table to enroll in their university. The donor collectives, however, ensure that there's transparency, NCAA compliance, and protection for both the donor and the student-athletes.

- **The marketplace collective:** This kind of collective plays a much more active role in helping the student-athletes pursue their NIL ambitions. These collectives have two sources of raising funds—one from the donors and the other from acting as agents for the athletes. The money received in donations can go into operating costs, which ensures that the collective remains profitable. These provide excellent networking opportunities, as they tend to have strong relationships with local and even national brands.

- **The dual collective:** This allows you to get the best of both worlds of marketplaces and donor collectives. This means that they can accept donations and also arrange for deals for student-athletes.

- **The YOKE collective:** This collective offers a technology-based solution that allows student-athletes to connect directly with their fans. The best part about these is that you get to be in charge of the collective, and you'd partner with YOKE for the technological infrastructure in exchange for 25% of their revenue. Partnerships can also happen between YOKE and the athletic departments of universities. This collective offers a software package with a website, mobile app, and admin dashboard, all of which help create a community-based approach to tapping into NIL opportunities.

Though collectives seem like wonderful opportunities for student-athletes, they also bring out some concerning conflicts in the athletic arena. It's important to note that though most universities have their own collectives (some more than one), the association isn't an official one, and truth is told; the NCAA isn't too pumped about collectives in general.

The apprehension began with a news report in *The Athletic* supplement of *The New York Times* (Mandel, 2022). This report brought to the fore the dark side of "pay-for-play," where a "five-star recruit in the Class of 2023" entered into a contract with a collective that would pay him more than $8 million by the end of his junior year, with $350,000 paid almost immediately. This, by no means, was an isolated incident, and the NCAA has had to look into multiple such cases since the arrival of NIL, and the settlements run in millions.

Despite these fallouts, however, most experts believe that collectives are here to stay. This is obvious when you pay attention to how far they have come from their amateurish setups. Take, for instance, the evolution of USC's Trojan athletics department. USC didn't have a collective to begin with, so it partnered with a third-party media agency called Stay Doubted to assist student-athletes with NIL opportunities. However, as the subsequent updates to the NCAA rules prohibited the universities from partnering with any entities negotiating with athletes on behalf of the universities, USC was forced to change its stance and eventually point the students to certain collectives, albeit unofficially.

The constantly evolving NCAA rules mean that the university-collective relationship is also changing all the time. Even though a university may have multiple collectives supporting it, the most effective collective initiatives have come to realize that their success depends on how in tune they are with the institutions they plan to support. Remember that though universities aren't allowed to offer student-athletes money to enroll, a 2024 court injunction prevents "the NCAA from enforcing any rule that prohibits student-athletes from negotiating compensation for NIL with any third-party entity, including but not limited to boosters or a collective of boosters." (Conniff *et al.*, 2024)

This means that collectives can and already have been negotiating deals with athletes well before their enrollment. Therefore, more and more collectives are turning into marketplaces that receive funds not only from supporters but also from the athletic departments of the universities.

Support and Beyond

The rise of NIL collectives has led to a seismic shift in the athletic recruitment landscape. That being said, recruiters aren't the only ones who benefit. These collectives create a win-win ecosystem for recruiters, universities, and, most importantly, student-athletes. Here are a few benefits that NIL collectives can bring to you:

- **Financial support:** NIL collectives can make life a lot easier for you by providing multifaceted financial assistance. Not only do you receive direct monetary compensation for your NIL, but these collectives also offer an excellent source of long-term financial stability. You may find that NIL collectives bring much more lucrative opportunities your way than individual negotiations, thus making for a higher earning potential. Moreover, the financial support provided by these collectives isn't limited only to better NIL opportunities; they also ensure that you're equipped with relevant financial resources such as financial literacy programs and financial advice.

- **Building brand value:** Collectives often have much higher leveraging power than individual student-athletes. As more and more brands are working toward diversity, equity, and inclusion, NIL collectives offer great platforms for student-athletes from all walks of life to connect with these brands. These collectives may just help you craft the perfect story for your brand, thereby helping you relate much better to the intended audience. Of course, you must be mindful of aligning with the right collective that resonates with your branding message to ensure that you reach a wider audience.

- **Business development resources:** An important aspect of NIL collectives is that they protect you from potential exploitation while making sure that you remain compliant with the NCAA rules. In addition to financial guidance, they also offer legal counsel, which is critical when you're trying to build a NIL business. You may also be able to access valuable resources such as mentorship programs, marketing expertise, and even connections with potential business partners.

Legal and Ethical Considerations

Shortly after the NIL rules came about, the LEAD1 association conducted a survey of athletic directors, in which 90% reported being concerned and 73% reported being extremely concerned about NIL payments being used for improper recruiting inducements both for high school prospects and transferring players (Auerbach, 2022). This is a staggering figure, to say the least.

Though NIL collectives have come a long way since then, the concerns still remain. I already mentioned the $8 million recruitment story that broke out in *The Athletic,* but unfortunately, this isn't the only story that raises suspicion about unscrupulous practices. Reports such as Texas's Clark Field Collective offering $50,000 to every Longhorns offensive lineman on scholarship or Built Brands providing free tuition for all of BYU's 36 walk-on players have been surfacing quite frequently (Planos, 2022). This is why legal and ethical considerations are of prime importance in the functioning of NIL collectives. Take a look at a few aspects that you must be mindful of when dealing with them:

- **Transparency:** In January 2024, the NCAA brought about a new rule (to be implemented by August 2024) regarding NIL transparency and disclosure, intending to "protect student-athletes by promoting the sharing and centralization of information related to NIL deals, such as contract terms and trustworthy service providers." (Reddy, 2024). This rule requires student-athletes to report any deals worth more than $600 to their schools. This information will then be de-identified and submitted to the NCAA to be further integrated into an aggregated database of all NIL deals.

  Though this centralization of data may be interpreted as intrusive, and, of course, the necessary steps must be taken to ensure that the student data remains protected, this may be a step in the right direction. While the ruling is intended only for student-athletes right now, it could potentially lead to the creation of a framework that brings much-needed transparency to the workings of universities, boosters, and collectives. Eventually, you may be able to look at the NCAA database to understand the trends in the NIL industry and proceed with deals that optimize your earning potential. With big bucks rolling in, this kind of transparency is bound to benefit everyone involved.

- **Conflict of interest:** You must understand that NIL collectives aren't charitable organizations that pour in money out of the goodness of their hearts. When you sign a contract with these collectives, they most certainly want something in return for the compensation they give you. Newcomers who lack contract negotiation experience and aren't yet familiar with how the markets operate can very well be taken advantage of if the collectives put their own financial interests ahead of the student-athletes they sign on. Contracts with collectives can also result in a significant reduction in your control over the brands you choose to endorse. Along with branding, you also want to be clear regarding the time commitments that are required of you for NIL endorsements and must ensure that these don't come in the way of your academic and athletic responsibilities.

- **Pay-for-play concerns and booster involvement:** Right since their arrival, the NIL rules have been shrouded in mystery, at least in parts. Some may even speculate that the evolving rules are inching closer and closer to pay-for-play. The injunction I mentioned earlier, which allows collectives to negotiate with student-athletes, is an excellent example of this movement. Even Charlie Baker, the NCAA president, has been vocal about allowing colleges to pay student-athletes for their NIL (McCann, 2024).

All said and done, considering the current status of the NCAA's NIL rules, pay-for-play still remains a touchy subject when it comes to NIL compliance. Therefore, before you sign any commitments with NIL collectives, you must have the highest possible clarity on what the NCAA rules permit at that point in time. Your NIL attorneys can be an invaluable resource in these instances and can steer you away from legally hazardous deals.

Partnering Strategically

Now that you know how beneficial and yet tricky the landscape of NIL collectives is, it's essential that you tread carefully. Even though NIL compliance rules can be overwhelming and confusing, there are certain steps you can take to ensure that your NIL deals offer you the maximum growth. Consider the following tips when dealing with the collectives:

- **Thorough research:** Certain NIL collectives may be great at luring student-athletes with excellent monetary offers. However, down the line, the student-athletes may realize that they've made a deal with the devil with excessive time and branding commitments. This is why it's paramount that you do the necessary research before signing any contracts. For basic information on the collective, you can visit the site *www.nilnewsstand.com/nil-collectives-database*, which allows you to search for NIL collectives by schools and conferences. Apart from this, you also want to ensure that the collective fulfills certain basic criteria:

    - An impeccable track record

    - Transparency in funding and operations

    - Reputation and goodwill

    - Alignment with your brand values and business goals

- **Professional guidance:** I've said this before, and I'll say it again: Navigating the maze of NIL rules and contracts on your own is neither easy nor recommended. It's crucial that you get the right help in the form of legal counsel who's well-versed in NIL compliance requirements and has an understanding of endorsement contracts. Only with this solid foundation will you be able to build an adaptable and successful business.

- **Long-term focus:** As commercial as the NIL space is, you must know that it's possible to connect with collectives who care about your growth. Try to find collectives that you can align with on a long-term basis and those that offer business development and other resources. Many of these may even provide mentorship programs. These can be the differentiators that make you stand out amongst the competition, and it may even be worth prioritizing them over the financial compensation that you end up receiving.

With this elaborate understanding of the NIL market, let's move on to understand how you can create a growth-oriented ecosystem of your own with a team that always has your back.

Chapter 8:

Building Your Team

In Chapter Four, we spoke a little about building your support system with not only your loved ones but professionals who help you further your career. Earlier, however, we only mentioned why those professionals would be important to your student-athlete entrepreneur journey. Now, let's delve a little deeper into the exact manner in which you can go about expanding your team to incorporate all of these critical pieces. This chapter helps you with practical tips on how to choose the best professionals and how they can help you transform your startup into an NCAA-compliant, lucrative enterprise.

Assembling the Dream Team

If you're an athlete, you're very familiar with the fact that your team can make or break the game for you. Of course, this is not some cliche way of passing on the blame, but the truth remains that no matter what happens, you and your team are in it together. Considering that even superheroes have their own teams to fall back on, you can safely say that having your own team may be your mantra to success. That being said, it's important to remember that your team can be your gateway to success *only* if it aligns with your branding and business value. If not, it can easily turn into your biggest liability.

This is why you must spend considerable time and effort handpicking the professionals who bring value to your journey. In this section, let's focus on three professionals who you might want to be extra careful about onboarding: financial advisors, legal counsel, and marketing experts.

Finding the Right Financial Advisors

With increasing awareness of financial literacy, more and more people understand the positive impact that a great financial advisor can create for their financial portfolio. This positive impact multiplies when you consider your journey from a student-athlete to an entrepreneur. A financial advisor can help you tighten your act in three specific areas:

- **Budgeting and cash flow management:** Believe it or not, being excellent at your sport and bringing the same excellence and discipline to your finances are two very different things. Not all fantastic athletes survive the world of entrepreneurship—this isn't because their business ideas are no good but because they just can't get a firm handle on their cash flow and budgeting needs. A good financial advisor has a knack for assessing your financial needs and helping you develop financial plans with realistic budgets that can help your business sustain itself and grow.

- **Tax planning and compliance:** Another pain point for many athletes (much like a large part of the general population) is finding their footing with the tax laws. Tax laws are often pretty complicated, and misunderstanding your tax obligations can have severe long-term consequences for yourself and for your business. What's worse is that the damage caused by these consequences can turn out to be more or less irreversible. This is why it's essential to ensure that you fulfill your obligations to Uncle Sam as thoroughly and accurately as possible. Your financial advisor plays a crucial role in helping you understand the tax implications of your business operations and ensure adherence to tax regulations.

- **Investment strategies:** Successful entrepreneurs know that building a business empire isn't just about earning more and more; what you do with those earnings is also equally important. With the right investing strategies, you can ensure that your money keeps growing even when you aren't working. This assumes special importance for you as a student-athlete entrepreneur, considering that you may or may not choose to stay an athlete after your education is completed. Even if you do remain an athlete, you aren't going to be hitting the field till you turn 70. This means that the investment portfolio you create today may help you live the life of your dreams, even if you decide to retire early. Having a financial advisor in your corner may help you explore potential investment options for your business and personal portfolio that align with your life vision.

Remember that you can do all of the above on your own, too, but perfecting each of these aspects may take years of experience, learning, and practice. So, why not leverage the help of a professional who's already at the top of their game in this area? Besides, enlisting a financial advisor to take care of your financial headaches means that you have more time and mental resources to focus on your athletic and business skills. Of course, that's not at all to say that you delegate financial responsibilities to the extent that you have no idea what's going on. But getting the right kind of help can take a lot of pressure off your mind.

That brings us to the ever-elusive question of *how* you can get the right help. Consider the following step-by-step procedure that can point you toward the best-aligned advisor:

Step #1: Take time to understand your own financial needs: Before you begin your hunt for the perfect financial advisor, take a moment and ask yourself a few questions:

- What do I expect from a financial advisor?

- Do I need them to help me with a budgeting plan for my personal and business expenses?

- Do I have any specific savings goals that I need help with?

- Do I need help with filing my tax returns? Do I have difficulty understanding the tax obligations for my business?

- Do I need them to help me with my investment portfolio?

- Do I want advice on the separation of personal and business finances?

Answering these questions will help you narrow down your exact requirements and will make the search much quicker and more effective.

Step #2: Explore the different types of financial advisors: As with everything else, the arrival of technology has greatly changed the landscape of financial awareness. Today, financial services may be utilized either traditionally on a face-to-face basis or in the form of an online service. Your answers to the above questions can help you choose one over the other. This is important because traditional financial advisors tend to have much higher fees than online financial services and may even have client eligibility criteria such as a minimum balance (sometimes up to $250,000). You can certainly consider these once you expand your business and your financial situation becomes more complex, but to begin with, online financial services may not be a bad option at all. If finding good investments is your only requirement, then you may even go for a robo-advisor, who will recommend an investment portfolio for you based on your goals and risk tolerance responses to an initial survey. This is the cheapest option, but it has the pitfall of not offering a complete financial plan. An online financial service, on the other hand, may give similar automated advice, but you may still be able to interact with a team of financial advisors online.

In addition to considering the above differences, you also want to make sure that you hire a fee-only financial planner and not a fee-based one. Fee-only planners have the fiduciary responsibility to put your interests above their own, which means they're bound by law to give you the best possible investment advice. On the other hand, fee-based advisors may receive commissions by selling you different financial products, which may motivate them to sell you things you may not need at all. Hiring financial planners for a flat fee is always recommended if your goal is to get financial advice on your current situation. Of course, if you want your advisor to manage your personal and business portfolio in the long run, then they're likely to charge you a percentage of your assets under management. Looking at these intricacies, you might be able to guess why it's important, first and foremost, to have clarity on your own requirements.

Step #3: Consider your own budget for hiring the advisor: As a student-athlete entrepreneur who may have a significant amount of funds tied up in the working capital for the business, cost remains a critical factor. How much can you afford to spare for financial services, considering all your other expenses? Here's a nifty comparison of varying financial advisor costs provided by NerdWallet (Coombes, 2024):

Fee type	Typical cost
Assets under management (AUM)	0.25% to 0.50% annually for a robo-advisor; 1% for a traditional in-person financial advisor.
Flat annual fee (retainer)	$2,000 to $7,500.
Hourly fee	$200 to $400.
Per-plan fee	$1,000 to $3,000.

Remember that these costs may again vary widely depending on where you're located and what your exact requirements are.

Step #4: Do thorough research on the advisor's background: Ask your friends and family for any recommendations they might have. Ensure that they have proper certifications and verify all the claims they make. You can check resources such as FINRA's BrokerCheck website or even their employment record to discover any red flags in their career. Make sure you have clear-cut answers to questions regarding their fiduciary status, the total costs of working with them, the tax implications, the extent of their accessibility and availability, their investment philosophy, and the investment benchmarks they use.

By following due diligence on all these steps, you can ensure that the financial advisor you choose is on the same wavelength as you.

What to Look For In Your NIL Legal Counsel

We've mentioned over and over how important legal counsel is in your NIL journey. However, to understand the exact role of an attorney in NIL deals, you must understand the step-by-step process for evaluating NIL deals. Here's a strategic framework you want to consider (Holon Law Partners, 2024):

- **Holistic assessment of the offer:** NIL offers come with several contingencies and intricacies, all of which you must be fully aware of before making any commitments. This is why you must ensure that the offer is evaluated in as much depth as possible. This specifically would include three things:

    o Going over the terms and conditions with a fine-tooth comb

    o Thoroughly researching the company's track record along with its legal legitimacy, market reputation, and so on

    o Ensuring that your brand vision and values are aligned with the overall company image as well as the specific deal they're offering

- **Valuation analysis:** NIL deals cannot be signed based on instinct; they must be supported by real-world numbers. Though we've mentioned several examples of deals worth millions, the unfortunate reality is that such deals aren't all that common. The available data from the NIL marketplace Opendorse shows that the average compensation per NIL deal is only about $1,300, and even this is likely to be inflated due to the much bigger deals, whereas other surveys suggest that the median compensation for Division I student-athletes was only about $65 per NIL activity (Carter, 2023). This isn't to disappoint or discourage you from pursuing NIL opportunities but rather to encourage you to vet the deals more thoroughly. Understand that valuation can vary widely based on factors such as athletic success, the strength of your brand, and its engagement with social media followers.

- **Risk mitigation:** As the NIL landscape is continuously evolving, there seem to be a lot of gray areas and loopholes that you need to be aware of. Taking a serious risk mitigation approach requires that you're able to identify aspects such as

    o compliance with the rules of the NCAA, your university, and state and federal laws.

    o exclusivity clauses that prevent you from pursuing other deals.

    o reputational damage that may come from legal and yet unethical or misleading products.

- **Strategic alignment:** We've spoken time and again regarding alignment between your brand and the offers you receive. But what does this mean in practical terms? Here are some things you can consider:

    o Does the deal prevent you in any way from meeting your athletic and academic responsibilities?

    o Does it leverage your skills and interests?

    o Does it expand your network and offer valuable professional experience outside of sports?

    o Does it contribute to your long-term vision?

- **Thoughtful negotiation:** Whenever you receive an offer from a company, it's safe to assume that the contract has been drawn, prioritizing the company's interests, not yours. Therefore, at this final stage, your goal would be to adjust it to ensure that your interests are protected equally. A few things that you must consider at this stage are as follows:

- **Intellectual property protections:** These safeguard your intellectual assets, such as name, image, and community platforms, with closely customized licensing.

- **Payment terms and conditions:** Think about the manner of payment disbursements that aligns most closely with your financial plan. Would you want to receive monthly payments rather than a lump sum? Would you want the payments based on your performance milestones? Remember that you get to have a say in these things, and you mustn't be afraid to exercise it.

- **Scope refinement:** Look for any ambiguous terms that may be used against you in the future. Make sure that the deliverables that are expected from you are precise and possible within your time commitments.

Though discussion on these can turn into contentious arguments, it's important that you try to reach win-win resolutions as far as possible. Remember that assertiveness is your friend in these negotiations, not aggression.

Now, based on this framework, it's easy to gauge why having legal counsel can prove extremely effective. An attorney who knows the ins and outs of NIL regulations can help you with three critical tasks, among everything else (Beaumont, 2024):

1. **Contract review and structuring:** Your lawyer can offer great insights when it comes to terms, merchandising rights, defining scope, and adding or removing waiver clauses and terminating conditions.

2. **Compliance:** Lawyers are in the best position to ensure that your contracts and compensation are compliant with NCAA and university requirements, in addition to any relevant laws.

3. **Legalities of brand partnerships:** A good NIL lawyer has an excellent grasp of IP rights, exclusivities, fee structures, and so on and can prevent you from signing disastrous deals.

Therefore, when you look for an NIL lawyer, you must ensure that they have adequate experience in the NIL landscape and accurate knowledge of the changing rules and regulations. But you might need to consider a little more than their expertise and skills. Since your interactions with your attorney are likely to be of a sensitive nature, abstract factors such as transparency and the personal connection that you feel with them may play a big role. Consulting the people in your sports network, such as fellow athletes, coaches, and so on, may help you score some good references. Even running a quick Google search will get you a long list of legal firms that claim to have NIL expertise. You may also check out the *NIL Network* website, which is a database where you can look for financial experts and legal counsel, among other resources. Whichever option you choose, be sure to vet it with thorough research, as you did with the financial advisor.

Onboarding the Perfect Marketing Experts

We've discussed branding in great detail throughout this book, and if you've paid attention, you'll know that marketing in itself is a full-time job. This means that, though you can kickstart it on your own, growing your brand is best executed as a team activity. That being said, a marketing expert is a broad term, and you must understand what these experts can do for your brand before you hire them. Here are a few traits that excellent market experts possess, and you shouldn't be hesitant to ask for these in your hired resources:

- **Experience:** You must look for a marketing expert who has worked in the NIL industry and is aware of general trends. Their broad range of experience makes them well-versed in the traditional or offline marketing and digital marketing channels that your brand may benefit from. Experienced market experts also know how to highlight their experience to attract the right customers. You'll be able to see their proficiencies on their own branding platforms, such as their website and social media profiles. Also, remember that these experts may not have the fanciest websites, but they may have ones that are error-free, efficient, and user-friendly.

- **Though lead generation:** Though your brand may benefit from offline marketing from time to time, the maximum traffic is likely to come from online channels. Therefore, you want to hire a company that has a great track record with online lead generation. The best way to understand if a marketing professional is a good fit for your NIL business is to ask them about how they plan to generate new leads (for instance, through search engine optimization, pay-per-click advertising, lead-generating tools such as websites that show pop-ups asking for emails, etc.). You also want to ask about the strategies that have worked most in the past, preferably with NIL clients. This will give you an idea of whether these professionals can walk the talk when it comes to using marketing to expand your business.

- **In-depth understanding of business challenges:** Good marketing experts ensure that they communicate clearly to understand your brand vision for the future as well as your perception of the current business challenges you face. This is where their experience working with NIL may also come to play a crucial role. They might even highlight aspects that you hadn't considered before. You may also want to work with someone who has collaborated with small businesses rather than big business empires. The idea here is that a marketing professional who has worked with small businesses will have a practical understanding of overcoming challenges with limited resources rather than running extravagant campaigns that may be outside your budget.

- **The knack for focusing on the most relevant business channels:** It's important to know that just because a particular type of marketing works for one athlete and their business doesn't mean it will work for you and your business. Good marketing professionals understand this fact very well and, therefore, try to figure out the channels that bring the highest returns for the lowest costs. For instance, a product that targets sports fans may do well to focus on social media platforms such as Instagram, YouTube, or Facebook, whereas a product that targets coaches may find better leads on LinkedIn. Your marketing expert should be able to help you narrow down the sweet spot that brings in the most traffic.

- **Exquisite testimonials and reviews:** Lastly, good marketing experts have glowing testimonials from their past clients. Not only do they highlight it, but they may also encourage you to get in touch with past clients who can share their positive experiences. If you don't want to get into too many marketing technicalities, this is your best shot at finding the right professional to collaborate with.

As you can see, these professionals are brilliant at creating a broad, customized marketing plan for your business that helps you build a stronger brand that resonates better with your target demographic.

When you onboard all these professionals and more, you create a team that's capable of assessing market changes and adapting effectively. While this is a massive part of leveraging your NIL rights, you also need to consider broadening your NIL ecosystem to truly tap into its maximum potential. This is where your brand partnerships come into play.

The Power of Partnerships

A business founded by a student-athlete entrepreneur may seem pretty niche in itself, but that may not be enough to create the differentiation that you're looking for. In a crowded market, partnering with the right brands can bring you massive traction. Consider the following benefits that partnering with the right brands can have for your business:

- **Enhanced credibility:** Collaborating with trusted and reputable brands can enhance your own credibility simply by association. If you were to partner with, let's say, an already beloved student-athlete alumnus who has created a brand of their own, your consumers would certainly have more faith in your brand. This is especially true for those who are on the fence about buying your product. Being endorsed by an established brand can give them just the nudge that encourages them to try it out, thus leading to much better conversion rates.

- **Expanded reach:** Branding with other partners that align with your values helps you tap into their existing customer base. For this, however, you just ensure that the brand you're partnering with has a similar target demographic as your brand. Such partnerships have the potential to give your audience numbers a great boost without expending excessive efforts and resources. This added visibility is fantastic for creating brand awareness.

- **Greater resources:** Partnering with established brands can give you access to brilliant insights about growing a business, innovative distribution channels, and even marketing challenges that your team may not have anticipated. These resources, though not tangible, have a big role to play in propelling your business further through more effective and strategic decision-making.

- **Better efficiency:** Strategic brand partnerships create win-win scenarios for both partners as they share resources, efforts, and even infrastructure costs to maximize the returns. For instance, brand partners can undertake joint marketing campaigns to reach a much wider audience, which means that their investment is essentially halved while doubling the output.

- **Long-term relationships:** Your brand exists in a market where the average consumer's attention span is shrinking while the competitive options are increasing by the minute. If long-term growth is your goal, then the only way to survive is to create trusting and lasting relationships geared toward mutual benefit. These strategic and diverse relationships offer you the flexibility and reassurance to navigate market uncertainties much more effectively.

Identifying and Negotiating Brand Partnerships

As great as brand partnerships are, identifying and negotiating them can prove challenging. While it's often tempting to want to partner with the most popular brand that you can reach, there are several other factors that you must consider. But before we get to those, it's important to know where to start. While social media is a wonderful channel to connect with other like-minded student-athlete entrepreneurs that you can collaborate with, be sure not to forget resources closer to home. For instance, if your university supports a strong athletic program, then it's very likely that you'll find athlete-entrepreneur alumni who have walked the path before you. You may even scour through your community resources to see if any of the members have created a business brand that you may want to partner with. Once you have these starting points, it's useful to know what to look for. We've mentioned this a few times already, but now, let's consolidate that information into a solid step-by-step guide to help you find the right brand partners.

Step #1: Have clearly defined goals: Before jumping into a collaboration with someone, you must be absolutely clear about your brand and business vision. However, this vision cannot be an abstract one. Remember the SMART goal-setting framework we discussed earlier? It's essential that you define your vision with clear, measurable metrics. Your goals may range from the audience size you plan to reach to your sales and revenue targets, lowering production costs, and so on within a defined timeframe. Only when you know these metrics like the back of your hand will you be able to narrow down the brand partners that will be able to help you improve specific metrics.

Step #2: Keep alignment at the core: Once you've defined your goal metrics, you need to focus on another equally important aspect—your brand values. What's your brand's mission statement and purpose? What kind of customer experience does your brand strive for? What aspects do you consider absolutely vital for the existence and growth of your brand? Defining these values makes life much easier for you, as it gives you a solid foundation on which to connect with others who share similar values. No matter how popular a brand is, if it doesn't align with your values, the benefits of such partnerships simply dissolve into nothingness.

Step #3: Consider the value they bring: Brand partnerships are excellent tools to fill the gaps in your business growth. When you engage in purposeful introspection about your goals and values, you will identify these gaps much more effectively. Think of these gaps as the holes and the partner's skills, expertise, and resources as the pegs that fill these holes. The best brand partnerships are the ones that bring complementary skills and resources together to create a distinctly formidable alliance that can stand out in a competitive market. Therefore, it's important that you're clear about the value that your partners bring to your growth in order to make the most of them.

Step #4: Understand their business approach: Though their skill is important, it's equally important that their style of functioning matches yours. You want to partner with someone who isn't afraid to innovate and has creative suggestions for collaboration. A brand partner who's rigid in their ways can be a tremendous burden despite the benefits that they may bring. Before committing to them, ensure that you have open and clear conversations with them regarding how they would like to proceed. Also, remember that there isn't one correct way of finding brand partnership success, and it's not about concluding that their business approach is better or worse than yours. It's only about finding the right fit, and understanding their workings is core to that.

Step #5: Research their background: If the prospective brand partner passes all the screening tests above, it's time to pull up your socks and thoroughly verify their background. What are the people saying about their brand online? How do they compare with other prospective partners? If you're collaborating with a student-athlete entrepreneur, ensure that they're compliant with the necessary regulations. Before partnering with another business, be sure to ask yourself, "Can I vouch for the quality and legitimacy of this brand with my own?" Because that's exactly what you'll be doing when you partner with them.

Once you've identified a potential partner, you'll then move on to negotiating a deal with them. Several negotiations break down because parties refuse to move from their initial demands and positions. So, how can you make sure that yours isn't one of them? Again, it's all about creating win-win scenarios, and here are a few negotiation principles that you can implement:

- **Understand that your interests are not the same as your positions:** Consider this story to understand the difference between interests and positions: Two individuals go to a grocery store to buy lemons. Unfortunately, all lemons are sold, but only one. The two individuals start arguing over who should get the last lemon. One says, "I want to make lemonade for my family!" The other says, "I want to use the lemon peels to make lemon-flavored cake for my wife." That is when both realize that their goal can easily be fulfilled, as one takes the peels for the cake and the other the lemon for the lemonade. Even though the two came to the store with the goal of buying lemons, they were still able to create a resolution that satisfied both parties.

- The trick is to differentiate between goals, which are your interests, and the means to getting to those goals, which is your position. Remember that there may be more than one way of getting to your goals, and thus, positions are negotiable, but interests are not. The more adamant you are about your positions, the more difficult negotiations become. Therefore, it's essential that you identify your ultimate goal and figure out if there is more than one way of getting to that goal.

- **Think about mutually beneficial resolutions:** When negotiating, it's not just your interests and positions that are important. Rather, you must try to understand the other party's positions and interests as well. Keeping the two sides in mind, you might be much better positioned to come to an alternative that serves both brands.

- **Don't confuse people with problems:** Negotiations often get heated because people take things quite personally. When you negotiate your partnership terms with other brands, there's bound to be some level of disagreement. It's important to remember that people don't disagree with you just for being difficult. Instead, they have their own views and perceptions. If the ultimate goal is problem resolution, then trying to understand the other's perspective empathetically is the only way.

- **Focus on objective criteria:** While your own metrics and facts are important, people may interpret them very differently. Focusing on these excessively can cause you or your partner to have polarized, entrenched views. Therefore, try to come up with clear objective deliverables for the partnership together.

- **Be clear about what you're willing to give up and what you aren't:** Before negotiating a brand partnership, you must be crystal clear about the scenario in which you'd be willing to walk away from a negotiation, no questions asked. Sure, you might be required to give up some of your demands, just as your negotiation partner would. But at the same time, you want to know what you aren't willing to compromise on.

Whether it's your team or your brand partnerships, they both nurture a collaborative ecosystem, and there's just a tad more to it in the form of mentors and networking.

Creating a Collaborative Ecosystem

The last two pieces of your entrepreneurial success puzzle are a mentor and the art of networking. Let's check out how these boost your growth.

Finding a Business Mentor

As an athlete, you know the role that your trainers and coaches play in all the improvements you've made in your technique so far. They offer you a unique analytical perspective on your game to ensure that you know what's working and what's not. That's the exact job that your business mentor would do. They challenge and question you in ways that make you reflect on your decision-making from the past and adjust it for higher efficiency in the future. Their extensive business experience and guidance can put you on a quicker path to success as you learn your lessons not only from their successes but also from their mistakes without actually making them yourself. A business mentor is a valuable asset for several reasons, but here are the three most critical ones:

- **Sounding board:** While you can certainly look to your mentors for advice when you run into difficulties, advice isn't all they give. Simply brainstorming about your situation with a trusted ally can give you the clarity and confidence to come up with effective resolutions.

- **Accountability:** Your business mentor can be your accountability partner who keeps you from straying away from your goals. In your entrepreneurial journey, you may frequently run into failure that overwhelms you and makes you give up. At such times, your mentor can pull you out of the depths of despair and encourage you to get back up and pursue your goals with new vigor.

- **Networking opportunities:** Lastly, their vast experience in the field also comes with several valuable connections that you can leverage. These connections may vary from those with people at the top, such as CEOs and industry leaders, to those at the grassroots who can help you get into the right places at the right time.

Of course, as advantageous as having a mentor is, good business mentors don't grow on trees. You might need to talk to multiple professionals before you feel that connection with someone. However, universities, business incubators, social platforms such as LinkedIn, or professional networking events in your community may all be great places to begin your search.

Building a Network

We've touched upon professional networking several times by now. So, what do you think about when I say networking? Most people think of some pretentious professionals in suits with sleazy hairstyles trying to convince people that their business is the next big thing! In other words, networking is often looked at as an opportunistic act of exchanging business cards in the hope that the other person will bring some kind of benefit to their business. Genuine networking, however, is far from this; much like negotiation, it's about arriving at win-win outcomes. Keep the following things in mind when you're networking with other athletes, entrepreneurs, industry professionals, and potential partners:

- **Focus on long-term relationships:** Networking is the long game, which means that the relationships you build may not give you immediate reward. Therefore, initiate a conversation and see where it goes. If it clicks, then ensure that you keep in touch by celebrating their successes and taking a genuine interest in their lives. It's these long-term relationships that will come to your aid when you least expect it.

- **Talk about what you have to offer:** Networking has come to have a sleazy reputation in many circles because everyone is always thinking about what they can get from the other person. Instead, think about the value you bring to the table and what you can do to help the other person. When you help them resolve their problem, they're much more likely to consider doing things for you in return the next time. Regardless, it's also crucial that you don't keep score.

- **Remember that quality is always better than quantity:** When you realize how important networking is for your business's success, it's natural to want to create as many connections as possible. But remember this: If you're constantly thinking of the next person you want to talk to, then you're never present in any conversations, which means no one has a reason to remember you after that conversation. Thus, rather than chatting up ten people at an event, you might as well have a genuine conversation with one person filled with questions about their life.

- **Follow up:** Lastly, no matter how authentic you thought a conversation was, the other person's busy life may simply drive you out of their mind within moments. Even if they remember you, they don't necessarily know what to do with that information. The best thing to do is to leave them a follow-up message or email with a personal touch. This doesn't mean you head straight to their social media profiles and add them as friends. That may be perceived as intrusive. The idea behind that message is only to throw the ball in their court, and they can now decide their next move.

Attending industry events, conferences, or workshops can be great opportunities for building valuable connections. Once you start using the above principles in combination with the communication tips discussed in Chapter 4, you'll start to experience the truly positive impact meaningful relationships can bring to your business's growth. As you already know, technology can serve as a great means of nurturing these relationships. However, this technology also serves a much wider function in the NIL landscape, which we shall explore in the next chapter.

Chapter 9:

Technology and Innovation in NIL

Considering that a large part of the NIL revolution is unfolding in the online world, it wouldn't be too far-fetched to say that technology is at the core of today's NIL movement. The implications of social media are obvious in drawing a successful NIL strategy. However, what you may not realize is that the strategic importance of this technology runs much deeper, and leveraging it in the right way can give you the ever-desired edge in the NIL market. This chapter aims to familiarize you with all things technology for your NIL success.

Tech Powering NIL

The first layer of technology that powers NIL is something we've discussed over and over—your social media profiles. Platforms like Instagram, TikTok, and Twitter remain the primary channels for athlete branding and NIL deals, especially due to their short-form content that audiences can scroll through quite quickly. In Chapter One, we've touched upon the various ways you can optimize your profiles through your content strategy. Now, let's take a slightly broader look at leveraging your social media with a big-picture view.

The Continued Dominance of Social Media

Social media in itself is an endless topic, which is why we've brought in several aspects of this means, such as strategic content, promotional advertising, and so on. Here, let's try to condense all we know about leveraging social media as a whole into a few practical and useful tips:

- **Learn which channels serve which sections of your target population:** Marketers often use the term "personas" to define specific segments of your target audience. So, even if your target demographic is men and women aged 18 to 35 years, this target will still have multiple segments, such as

  - o   Persona A male/female teenager studying in college

  - o   Persona B who is a working individual 23–27 years old

  - o   Persona C who is a working parent

  These are very basic personas that I've mentioned solely for the purpose of understanding, but they should help you see that different parts of your target demographic have very different priorities, needs, wants, and goals. Therefore, it's only logical to assume that they're all interacting with you through different social media platforms. For instance, data shows that 32.5% of TikTok's user base is between 10 and 19 years old, whereas 33.1% of global Instagram audiences are in the age range of 25 to 34 years (Needle, 2020). This is a critical insight that must inform your social media strategy, with your content optimized for diverse channels.

- **Focus on getting engagement and community-building:** Posts that show your athletic schedules, quirky personalities, business challenges, and so on are obviously great for creating a brand that builds your fan base and attracts potential brand partners. However, that may not always be enough to build the traction that your business requires. Your followers are always looking for something more, and targeting engagement may just do the trick. This can be achieved in several ways:

  - o   Hashtags

  - o   Contests and giveaways

  - o   Polls and surveys

  - o   Creating shareable and relatable content

o   Posting more video content

Using these tools (and more), you can create compelling social media posts that foster a feeling of community in your followers, which in turn may create brand loyalty like nothing else.

- **Have a solid sales plan in place:** It's crucial to remember that being on top of your social media game isn't the goal in itself but rather a means to an end, which is growing your business. In some cases, you may create the product yourself, whereas in others, you may be selling a tangible product that you create or distribute. Whichever it is, your sales strategy becomes a top priority. To do this, you must have a strong grasp of what marketers like to call the buyer's journey:

  o   **Awareness:** The buyer becomes aware that there's a problem, although they haven't yet reflected on it too much.

  o   **Emails:** They start defining the problem and start actively looking for solutions.

  o   **Decision:** They've evaluated multiple options and finally decided to opt for the best.

On your social media channels, you must provide a mix of content that addresses all of these stages. To help them get to the last stage and eventually make the purchase. You also want to have a clear plan for generating the right leads, and nudging them toward your brand without spamming them with emails.

- **Integrate customer service with your social media:** Customer service is one of the biggest factors that consumers consider, and ignoring that in your social media strategy would be an opportunity missed. Statistics suggest that 59% of global social media users view those brands that respond to customer service questions on social media more favorably (Needle, 2020). You don't need to answer all of their questions on Instagram or X, but even politely directing them to preferred channels such as mail or call can let them know that you're responsive and care about what they have to say.

- **Utilize the power of data analytics:** Social media without data analysis tools may be very similar to a toy in a child's hands. Not only do these help you understand your audience engagement, but they can also help you modify your content and posting strategy, right from the type of content to the timing of positioning, to generate more traffic. Without proper emphasis on these metrics, you can be sure that your competition will always have an edge over you in offering relevant and relatable content and products. Since customer engagement is the most important factor in your NIL deals, this can turn into a major hurdle in your path.

Empowering Athletes With New Tools

Think of technology powering NIL as onion layers; the more you peel, the more you realize there is. If we think of social media as the first layer, then the several tools discussed in this section could easily be the deeper second layer. These might not be very obvious at first glance, but they often end up becoming your entry points to the lucrative world of NIL. Take a look:

- **NIL marketplaces:** NIL marketplaces are platforms that connect student-athletes with brands. There are several great NIL marketplaces that you can check out (Clapper, 2023):

  - PlayBooked

  - MOGL

  - Open Sponsorship

  - OpenDorse

  - PostGame

o   NOCAP

o   IconSource

The biggest benefit that these marketplaces offer is that you can choose from a buffet of campaigns, and if the brand thinks you're a good fit, then you proceed with the deal. This makes for a great medium to work with brands that are actively looking to work with student-athletes and expand your NIL portfolio. Of course, these aren't the only sources of NIL deals, and the bigger deals often happen outside of such marketplaces. That being said, they're a great starting point for your NIL career.

The popularity of these marketplaces is on the rise, and their offerings are constantly evolving. For instance, CollectID is an NIL marketplace that offers what's known as "phygital technology," which is a blend of physical and digital user experiences (Foley, 2023). So, let's say a brand partners with an athlete and decides to release some athlete merchandise for the fans. While this constitutes the physical experience, the platform also has its digital perks for its end-users, such as behind-the-scenes updates about their favorite athletes, giveaways organized by branding partners, and so on. While the universities and the athletes find better compensation opportunities and increased fan engagement, the fans get tangible rewards and intangible perks.

- **Fan engagement apps:** As can be seen above, fan engagement is a big driver in the NIL industry. Therefore, it's obvious that technology has evolved to enhance not only the experience of brands and student-athletes but also the ever-crucial fans. Fan engagement apps are at the forefront of this movement. What's more, these fan apps aren't created only for entertainment but come with great benefits for fans, such as personalized and exclusive content, real-time updates regarding their favorite sports and athletes, access to tickets and merchandise, and so on. However, fans aren't the only ones that benefit. Student-athletes and brands have a lot to gain, too.

Consider the following benefits that fan apps may bring for you
:

- o **Valuable consumer behavior insights:** Fan apps are your direct connection with your fans with no middlemen. This means that you can get a real read on your fans' behavior with metrics such as usage patterns and in-app activities. These data points are particularly crucial, as they tell you what your fans are really interested in. This can create a strong foundation for effective and strategic decision-making regarding marketing and expanding your brand.

- o **Personalized offerings:** With the above insights, you can curate personalized fan experiences that create a sense of exclusivity in your fan's psyche. This exclusivity can be a fantastic catalyst to strengthen the bond you have with your fans, which eventually leads to their unwavering brand loyalty.

- o **Sponsorship activations:** Let's say an app reveals that a certain fan base is extremely interested in health and nutrition, then it turns into an attractive prospect for nutrition brands and thus activates sponsorships from that industry segment.

- o **Feedback loop:** These apps are a great source for opening feedback channels that connect fans with brands and athletes directly. This not only allows you to make adjustments to your marketing and overall business approach but also lets your fans know that their voice matters.

There are several fan engagement apps that you might want to check out (WowTalkies, 2023):

- o JumpTrade

- o Striker Club

- o SportzChain

- o Socios

- o Greenfly

- o Dugout

- o FanThreeSixty

As you can see, whether it's NIL marketplaces or fan engagement apps, the ultimate goal is to leverage your NIL rights to monetize fan engagement and create mutually beneficial experiences for all stakeholders. These platforms often use advanced technology to create wholesome experiences for their users, which brings us to the last layer of technology. Sure, these forms are still in their infancy, but they may just shape the future of NIL and are thus, worth every bit of your time.

The Future of NIL

Several emerging technologies are being experimented with in different sections of the NIL landscape. However, blockchain technology is one form of technology that offers great promise for any student-athlete who wishes to leverage their NIL rights effectively.

I know blockchain sounds like a fancy, complicated technical term, but stay with me for just a moment. Don't worry; we won't get into the technicalities too much, but it's still important that you understand the basics to leverage it in the best way possible. Blockchain is a shared digital ledger that maintains a growing amount of data in the form of "blocks."

What's special about this form of technology is that the data is stored in a decentralized and transparent fashion but is completely immutable, which means it cannot be falsified. In other words, anyone can view the stored data, but no one can modify it. But why does this matter? Simple because it offers security, traceability, and transparency, which fosters a sense of trust, especially where monetary transactions are concerned.

Now, you might be wondering how this matters to you and your NIL career. Well, the truth is that many of the platforms discussed above already use blockchain technology. These platforms offer yet another profitable avenue for athletes, as they allow them to create their own digital assets and monetize them. Essentially, you're no longer dependent only on endorsement deals but can create your own revenue stream, which can support you for a long time. To tap into its full potential, you might want to understand two specific aspects:

- **NFTs:** Non-fungible tokens are unique assets created on a blockchain and can garner massive wealth for you. Their value lies in the fact that they aren't fungible or interchangeable with anything else. Imagine this: You have a ten-dollar note, and I have two fivers. You can easily exchange your one note with two of mine because they're exchangeable. On the other hand, if you create a piece of art, music, video, or any form of digital content, it would be non-fungible and one of a kind. Remember, NFTs have no tangible form and are completely virtual. So, rather than handing over your work to a buyer, you'd retain the copyrights of the piece and can create and sell copies, creating a strong revenue stream. Additionally, since you hold the copyright, you may even earn significant royalties.

- **Cryptocurrencies:** People often use Bitcoin and cryptocurrency synonymously, but remember that Bitcoin is only one (and the most prolific) type of cryptocurrency. You can think of these as the fungible version of NFTs. Cryptocurrencies are also digital assets created on blockchains that offer secure and transparent transactions, and this can be quite valuable as a form of payment in NIL deals. However, this is still in its early stages, and there are substantial challenges to consider.

Challenges and Considerations

As wonderful as blockchains are, the digital assets created on them come with several challenges:

- **Volatility:** The prices of digital assets can fluctuate a great deal over brief periods of time. This means that you can either harvest massive rewards or risk a significant dip in your investment value.

- **Regulation:** Since digital assets come with a decentralized but anonymous framework, authorities have frequently faced intense regulatory challenges. So, if you run into any complications after investing in them, you may not have any legal recourse.

- **Security:** While transactions with digital assets are highly secure, their storage is often the tricky part. These assets are stored in a digital wallet on the blockchain and require a combination of public and private keys. The challenge is that the private key that remains with you isn't retrievable. This means that losing your key leads to a complete loss of the digital assets you hold, and they can never be accessed again.

Apart from these, there's also the challenge of getting all stakeholders to adopt this technology, leaving the traditional methods as the more popular choice for the current times. However, I still urge you to stay updated on these evolving trends so that you can be prepared for anything that comes your way. For now, let's consolidate all of the resources that we've touched upon so far in the last chapter.

Chapter 10:

Resources

By now, you have gained a fair bit of clarity on your NIL rights and the best possible ways to leverage them. Now, let's take the final step of equipping you with a few resources that will help you in your NIL journey.

Financial Literacy Websites

Note that there are several financial literacy websites out there, but you need to ensure that you get your information from the most trusted sources.

- The National Endowment for Financial Education (*www.nefe.org*)

- The U.S. Securities and Exchange Commission (*www.investor.gov*)

- Khan Academy Personal Finance Course (*www.khanacademy.org*)

Financial Planning Apps

Financial planning apps can either be free or paid. They may have varying features, and you must choose the ones that suit your individual needs the best. If you go for the paid versions, be sure to take advantage of their free trial to ensure that they fulfill your requirements.

Free Apps

- Mint

- Goodbudget

- Personal Capital

- Empower

Paid Apps

- YNAB (You Need A Budget)

- Simplifi

- Rocket Money

Tax Resources

While it's always recommended that you consult a tax advisor, you must also be updated with the latest IRS guidelines.

- Internal Revenue Service (IRS) website (*www.irs.gov*)

NIL Compliance Resources

This is the best resource to get you information about all things NCAA and NIL.

- The National Collegiate Athletic Association (NCAA) website (*www.ncaa.org*)

NIL Legal Resources

These organizations advocate for athlete rights and provide legal resources related to NIL.

- National Fair Play Alliance (*www.fairplayalliance.org*)

- Athletes First Alliance (*www.athletesfirst.net*)

Sample Business Plans

Here are two templates to get you started on your business plan. Fill these out as you deem fit. These are just two business ideas that may be relevant to athlete-entrepreneur business models. Feel free to add to these ideas.

Athlete-Branded Apparel Line

- **Executive Summary:** Briefly outline your vision, target market, and competitive advantage.

- **Products and Services:** Describe your apparel line, including product design, materials, and pricing.

- **Marketing Strategy:** Explain how you plan to leverage your NIL rights and social media presence to market your apparel line.

- **Financial Projections:** Provide an overview of your projected sales, costs, and profitability.

- **Management Team:** Introduce yourself and any partners or advisors involved in your business.

Online Fitness Training Program

- **Executive Summary:** Briefly outline your fitness program concept, target audience, and unique selling proposition.

- **Training Programs:** Describe the types of fitness programs you offer, including workout routines, target areas, and pricing models.

- **Digital Platform:** Explain how you plan to deliver your training programs (e.g., mobile app, online subscription platform).

- **Marketing Strategy:** Detail how you plan to reach your target audience and promote your online fitness programs.

Conclusion

There you go—everything you need to know about NIL to begin your entrepreneurial journey right away. I bet you're ready to get started, too. NIL offers infinite exciting possibilities for growth, after all. What's more, it's not just about building successful businesses but also strong personal brands and legacies that can inspire people for years to come. But, now, you also know that NIL success is a lot more than just following the NCAA rules.

We've tackled a lot of information in this book, and it can be quite overwhelming to take it all in at once. I recommend that you keep this as a handy reference that you return to whenever you feel lost. Also, keep in mind that the purpose of this book was to give you a compact version of all that you need to know about NIL. This is only a starting point, and you may have to take on more advanced books on specific topics of marketing, branding, and so on. Despite its compact nature, if you still feel overwhelmed, then focus your attention on three key areas:

#1: Yourself: You are an asset, and you need to nurture your value. Your business and branding efforts will stick only if they are centered around what matters to you.

#2: Rules and regulations: Remaining compliant with the NCAA's changing NIL landscape is the only way to survive and succeed.

#3: Your ecosystem: Spend time and effort building genuine, long-term relationships with people, and you'll not be disappointed.

Work on these three facets, and you'll shine no matter what business you choose.

All said and done, entrepreneurship also comes with a certain amount of uncertainty and discomfort. It requires that you break away from your comfort zone, and that can be the hardest task of all. So, take that first step and go visit the resources mentioned in the last chapter to find your path.

If you found this book to be helpful, make sure you leave a review. It will help me reach more student-athlete entrepreneurs who don't know where to start. As for your journey, I wish you courage, perseverance, and success on this new adventure you're about to embark on. All the best!

Want more reads like this or readings about entrepreneurship?
Teens, Athletes & Entrepreneurs. Visit StudstillCo Online Store by
going to https://payhip.com/StudstillCo and click on "Join Our
Mailing" to stay updated on exclusive consulting, special offers for new
books and courses, and transformative insights. Don't miss out on the
opportunity to be part of a community dedicated to innovation and
cosmic exploration.

If you enjoy this book, can you give the author a review? Please
visit www.amazon.com/author/johnnystudstilljr

References

ActiveCollab Team. (2024, May 13). *Pareto principle for time management and prioritization.* ActiveCollab. https://activecollab.com/blog/project-management/pareto-principle

Alexander, M. (2023, April 7). *How to make financial projections for business.* FreshBooks. https://www.freshbooks.com/hub/finance/financial-projections

Ambler, W. (2024, January 31). *Report: 2024 sports trends & predictions.* Catapult. https://www.catapult.com/blog/2024-sports-trends-predictions-report

Armato, L. (2024, February 26). *NIL court loss: NCAA must embrace pay for play to survive. see how.* Forbes. https://www.forbes.com/sites/leonardarmato/2024/02/26/big-nil-court-loss-means-ncaa-must-embrace-pay-for-play--to-survive/?sh=48e5a4f56284

Athlete service provider directory. (n.d.). NIL Network. https://www.nilnetwork.com/nil-company-directory-athletes/NIL-Company-Industry/athlete-nil-services/legal-services/

Auerbach, N. (2022, May 4). FBS ADs "extremely concerned" by collectives. *The New York Times.* https://www.nytimes.com/athletic/3499920/2022/05/04/college-leaders-extremely-concerned-with-nil-collectives-direction-survey/

AWM Capital. (2022, April 7). *NIL rules explained: How to stay NCAA compliant and profit off your NIL.* AWM. https://awmcap.com/blog/nil-rules

Barron, B. (2023, April 27). *Why schedule social media posts ahead of time?* Jetpack. https://jetpack.com/blog/schedule-social-media-posts

Beaumont, C. (2024, February 12). *Finding the right lawyer for an NIL deal.* Total Football Analysis. https://totalfootballanalysis.com/opinion/finding-the-right-lawyer-for-an-nil-deal

Bleichner, T. (2022, September 11). *NIL program comparison at universities.* NIL Network. https://www.nilnetwork.com/nil-program-comparison/

Britannica. (2024). *National collegiate athletic association.* https://www.britannica.com/topic/National-Collegiate-Athletic-Association

Brown, M. (2024, March 4). *How NIL collectives can not suck at NIL.* Extra Points. https://www.extrapointsmb.com/p/nil-collectives-can-not-suck-nil

Bullock, A., & Dahman, S. (2024, March 7). *Student athletes secure victory over NCAA: Discussing the future of NIL in collegiate athletics.* JD Supra. https://www.jdsupra.com/legalnews/student-athletes-secure-victory-over-1801100/

Business plan executive summary. (2024, April 26). Examples.com. https://www.examples.com/business/business-plan-executive-summary.html

Cardoso, P. (2022, July 6). *Inky johnson biography, family, career, wife, history, net worth.* Buzz. https://www.naijanews.com/buzz/people/inky-johnson-biography-family-career-wife-heritage-measurements/

Carter, B. (2023, January 17). *Seven data points that will tell the story of NIL in 2023.* Sports Business Journal. https://www.sportsbusinessjournal.com/SB-Blogs/OpEds/2023/01/17-Carter.aspx

CFI Team. (n.d.). *Cash flow statement template.* https://corporatefinanceinstitute.com/resources/financial-modeling/cash-flow-statement-template/

Chapman, S., & Rupured, M. (2024, February 19). *Time management: 10 strategies for better time management.* University of Georgia Extension. https://extension.uga.edu/publications/detail.html?number=C1042&title=time-management-10-strategies-for-better-time-management

Clapper, L. (2023a, March 23). *Do I need an LLC for NIL deals?* NIL Island. https://nilisland.com/do-i-need-an-llc-for-nil-deals/

Clapper, L. (2023b, March 23). *The best NIL marketplaces to sign up for.* NIL Island. https://nilisland.com/the-best-nil-marketplaces-to-sign-up-for

Conniff, C. P., Coleman, D. M., Han, E. L., Oteh, C., Freshman, D., Little, W. (Will) E. A., Wheeler, T., De La Torre, E. M., & Gondalia, P. (2024, February 15). *NIL round-up: New NCAA DI student-athlete protections, policy proposals, enforcement actions, and the current state of NIL.* Ropes & Gray. https://www.ropesgray.com/en/insights/alerts/2024/02/nil-round-up-new-ncaa-di-student-athlete-protections-policy-proposals-enforcement-actions

Coombes, A. (2024a, April 26). *10 questions to ask a financial advisor.* NerdWallet. https://www.nerdwallet.com/article/investing/10-questions-ask-financial-advisor

Coombes, A. (2024b, April 26). *How much does a financial advisor cost?* NerdWallet. https://www.nerdwallet.com/article/investing/how-much-does-a-financial-advisor-cost

Cote, C. (2022, April 5). *How to identify business & market opportunities.* Harvard Business School - Business Insights Blog. https://online.hbs.edu/blog/post/how-to-identify-business-opportunities

Coursera. (2024a, March 27). *Market analysis: What it is and how to conduct one.* https://www.coursera.org/articles/market-analysis

Coursera. (2024b, April 4). *Marketing strategy: What it is and how to create one.* https://www.coursera.org/articles/marketing-strategy

Create engaging and effective social media content. (2024, May 5). Hootsuite. https://help.hootsuite.com/hc/en-us/articles/4403597090459-Create-engaging-and-effective-social-media-content#know-your-post-anatomy-0-0

Creating a positive public image by registering your business for startups. (2024, April 10). FasterCapital. https://fastercapital.com/content/Creating-a-Positive-Public-Image-by-Registering-Your-Business-for-Startups.html#How-to-Maintain-Your-Positive-Public-Image-.html

Daugherty, G. (2024a, February 27). *What is NIL? Understanding name, image, and likeness rules.* Investopedia. https://www.investopedia.com/name-image-likeness-8558991

Daugherty, G. (2024b, March 7). *NIL and the NCAA: What are the rules?* Investopedia. https://www.investopedia.com/nil-and-the-ncaa-8599762

Dellenger, R. (2024, May 28). *The next evolution of NIL collectives and the battles that await: "This is a big inflection point."* Yahoo Sports.

https://sports.yahoo.com/the-next-evolution-of-nil-collectives-and-the-battles-that-await-this-is-a-big-inflection-point-120051261.html

Diaz, N. M. (2024, March 12). *Master the STAR method: Tips, questions & answer examples.* My Perfect Resume. https://www.myperfectresume.com/career-center/how-to-use-the-star-method

Dodd, D. (2022, May 10). *Boosters, collectives in NCAA's crosshairs, but will new NIL policy be able to navigate choppy waters?* CBS Sports. https://www.cbssports.com/college-football/news/boosters-collectives-in-ncaas-crosshairs-but-will-new-nil-policy-be-able-to-navigate-choppy-waters/

Drew. (2023, March 10). *How do collegiate NIL collectives work?* Crown, LLP. https://crownllp.com/blog/how-do-collegiate-nil-collectives-work/

11 tips to build a social media presence. (n.d.). Birmingham City University. https://www.bcu.ac.uk/business-school/blog/eleven-tips-to-build-a-social-media-presence

Fan apps: Revolutionizing the sports experience. (n.d.). Crowdmanager. https://crowdmanager.io/fan-apps-in-sport

Fenaroli, P. (2024, March 11). *Navigating the new frontier: The rise of NIL collectives in college sports - pastore.* Pastore. https://www.pastore.net/navigating-the-new-frontier-the-rise-of-nil-collectives-in-college-sports/

Fernando, J. (2024, January 31). *Balance sheet: Explanation, components, and examples.* Investopedia; Investopedia. https://www.investopedia.com/terms/b/balancesheet.asp

5 athletes succeeding in business. (2021, August 13). Athlete365. https://olympics.com/athlete365/career/5-athletes-succeeding-in-business/

5 key benefits of student-athletes going to an NCAA school. (2023, June 26). U.S Sports Scholarships. https://www.ussportsscholarships.com/benefits-of-ncaa/

The 5 most common pricing strategies. (n.d.). BDC. https://www.bdc.ca/en/articles-tools/marketing-sales-export/marketing/pricing-5-common-strategies

The 5 Step Process for Securing Your NIL Rights as a Student-Athlete. (2023, November 8). Holon Law Partners. https://holonlaw.com/2023/the-5-step-process-for-securing-your-nil-rights-as-a-student-athlete/

Foley, T. (2023, May 16). *Revolutionizing NIL deals: How collectID technology empowers brands and college athletes.* Zatap. https://zatap.io/creating-win-win-partnerships-brands-and-athletes-in-the-nil-era/

Foo, S. (2020, May 27). *37 inspiring branding quotes from billionaires & CEOs.* SpeechSilver. https://speechsilver.com/branding-quotes/

For student-athletes to succeed, the NCAA must be held accountable. (2024, February 26). U.S. Senator Marsha Blackburn of Tennessee. https://www.blackburn.senate.gov/2024/2/for-student-athletes-to-succeed-the-ncaa-must-be-held-accountable

Forsey, C. (2023, August 31). *How to write a powerful executive summary [+4 top examples].* Hubspot. https://blog.hubspot.com/marketing/executive-summary-examples

Franchise partnership: Franchise partnerships: Expanding your business horizons. (2024, April 12). FasterCapital. https://fastercapital.com/content/Franchise-Partnership--Franchise-Partnerships--Expanding-Your-Business-Horizons.html#Exploring-the-Power-of-Franchise-Partnerships.html

Free income statement template. (n.d.). FreshBooks. https://www.freshbooks.com/accounting-templates/income-statement

Frieser, J. (2022, November 2). *A comprehensive legal guide for NIL industry start-ups.* Frieser Legal. https://frieserlegal.com/a-comprehensive-legal-guide-for-nil-industry-start-ups/

From running back to entrepreneur. (2024). Kent State University. https://www.kent.edu/foreverbrighter/news/running-back-entrepreneur

Full-Court vision: How legal counsel can help student-athletes navigate NIL deals. (2021, August 17). Barton LLP. https://www.bartonesq.com/news-article/full-court-vision-how-legal-counsel-can-help-student-athletes-navigate-nil-deals/

Geyser, W. (2024, January 30). *What is the best length for social media posts? (Free character counter).* Influencer Marketing Hub. https://influencermarketinghub.com/best-length-for-social-media-posts/

GiftsToGive. (2012, June 15). *Empty pickle jar.* Vimeo. https://vimeo.com/44102006

Gough, C. (2024, April 18). *Sports industry revenue worldwide in 2022, with a forecast for 2028(in billion U.S. dollars).* Statista. https://www.statista.com/statistics/370560/worldwide-sports-market-revenue

Hague, P. (2006). *A practical guide to market research.* https://www.b2binternational.com/assets/ebooks/mr_guide/practical-guide-to-market-research_full.pdf

Herrity, J. (2023, March 11). *What does it mean to be professional?* Indeed Career Guide. https://www.indeed.com/career-advice/career-development/what-does-it-mean-to-be-professional

Hodgkins, J. (2022, October 8). *4 steps to building your brand: How student-athletes can win with NIL.* Darden Ideas to Action. https://ideas.darden.virginia.edu/build-your-brand-student-athletes#footnote1_p3ihf03

Holon Law Partners. (2024, January 4). *The 5-step process for evaluating NIL offers.* https://holonlaw.com/the-5-step-process-for-evaluating-nil-offers/

Hough, Q. (2024, June 6). *Top 10 best college athletic programs in the U.S.* WatchMojo. https://www.watchmojo.com/articles/top-10-best-college-athletic-programs-in-the-u-s/university-of-alabama

Hutchings, V. (2021, January 22). *How to conduct market research for your business idea.* Tide Business. https://www.tide.co/blog/business-tips/market-research/

iGrad Author. (2024, May 29). *How schools can help student-athletes navigate the financial details of NIL.* IGrad for Schools. https://www.igradfinancialwellness.com/blog/how-schools-can-help-student-athletes-navigate-the-financial-details-of-nil

Indeed. (2023, January 27). *Market needs: What they are and 9 strategies to define them.* https://www.indeed.com/career-advice/career-development/market-needs

Indeed Editorial Team. (2022, June 25). *Marketing's promotional mix: Definition and how to use it.* Indeed Career Guide.

https://www.indeed.com/career-advice/career-development/marketing-promotional-mix

Indeed Editorial Team. (2023, October 16). *How to create a balance sheet in 5 steps (with examples).* https://www.indeed.com/career-advice/career-development/how-to-make-a-balance-sheet

Indeed Editorial Team. (2024, April 29). *What is a business advisor? (With skills and duties).* https://in.indeed.com/career-advice/finding-a-job/what-is-a-business-advisor

Insight. (2024, January 23). *Here's a look at what's in store for the 2024 US sports nutrition market, plus key trends and opportunities—like weight loss-positioned products and cleaner pre-workout energy drinks.* Glanbia Nutritionals. https://www.glanbianutritionals.com/en/nutri-knowledge-center/insights/us-sports-nutrition-outlook

Jeremy. (2023, June 30). *Understanding how NIL collectives work.* RootNote. https://rootnote.co/understanding-how-nil-collectives-work/

Johnson, J. (2019, February 25). *Sizing up the competition: How to conduct competitive research.* U.S. Chamber of Commerce. https://www.uschamber.com/co/start/strategy/how-to-conduct-competitive-research

Johnson, S. R., Wojnar, P. J., Price, W. J., Foley, T. J., Moon, J. R., Esposito, E. N., & Cromartie, F. J. (2011, February 14). *A coach's responsibility: Learning how to prepare athletes for peak performance.* The Sport Journal. https://thesportjournal.org/article/a-coachs-responsibility-learning-how-to-prepare-athletes-for-peak-performance/

Kenton, W. (2024, January 30). *Marketing mix: The 4 ps of marketing and how to use them.* Investopedia. https://www.investopedia.com/terms/m/marketing-mix.asp

Kruse, K. (2016, May 7). *The 80/20 rule and how it can change your life*. Forbes. https://www.forbes.com/sites/kevinkruse/2016/03/07/80-20-rule/?sh=5a0af1f13814

Lens, J. (2023, April 17). *NIL compliance*. Boston University Law Review. https://www.bu.edu/bulawreview/2023/04/17/nil-compliance/

Levine, L., & Person, M. (2014, May 28). *10 ways to authentic and genuine networking* . JuiceTank. https://www.juicetank.com/authentic-genuine-networking-tips/

Lynam, A. R., & Smith, P. (2024, March 13). *When one (NCAA) door closes, another (NIL) door opens: What pre-collegiate enrollment NIL deals mean for schools & NIL collectives*. Montgomery McCracken Walker & Rhoads LLP. https://www.mmwr.com/when-one-ncaa-door-closes-another-nil-door-opens-what-pre-collegiate-enrollment-nil-deals-mean-for-schools-nil-collectives/

Lyons, K. (2023, December 18). *A beginner's guide to online reputation management*. Semrush Blog. https://www.semrush.com/blog/online-reputation-management

MacNeil, C. (2024, January 12). *Try these 12 promotion strategies to create customer demand*. Asana. https://asana.com/resources/promotion-strategy

Mandel, S. (2022, March 12). Five-star recruit in Class of 2023 signs agreement with collective that could pay him more than $8 million. *The Athletic*. https://www.nytimes.com/athletic/3178558/2022/03/11/five-star-recruit-in-class-of-2023-signs-agreement-with-collective-that-could-pay-him-more-than-8-million/

Marcene, B. (2023, April 21). *25 small business ideas for athletes and sports lovers*. ASBN America's Small Business Network. https://www.asbn.com/start-a-business/entrepreneurship/25-small-business-ideas-for-athletes-and-sports-lovers/

Market Me Consulting. (2023, May 4). *Tips for choosing the right brand partner in 2023*. LinkedIn. https://www.linkedin.com/pulse/tips-choosing-right-brand-partner-2023-marketmeja/

Market research questions: What to ask and how. (2022, April 5). Qualtrics. https://www.qualtrics.com/au/experience-management/research/market-research-questions/

Marr, B. (2023, April 5). *Fit for the future: 10 trends that will transform the fitness industry*. Forbes. https://www.forbes.com/sites/bernardmarr/2023/04/05/fit-for-the-future-10-trends-that-will-transform-the-fitness-industry/?sh=5717338b4000

Martin, J. (2020, June 10). LeBron James and other stars form a voting rights group. *The New York Times*. https://www.nytimes.com/2020/06/10/us/politics/lebron-james-voting-rights.html

Massonos, C. (2019, October 16). *Recommended social media platforms for athletes*. Money Smart Athlete Blog. https://moneysmartathlete.com/the-athletes-brand/recommended-social-media-platforms-for-athletes/

McCann, M. (2024, April 8). *Direct NIL Payments Could Be Final Nail in Amateurism's Coffin*. Sportico. https://www.sportico.com/law/analysis/2024/direct-nil-payments-colleges-ncaa-1234774185/

Messineo, N. (2023, November 21). *Emergence of student-athlete entrepreneurs creates new market for attorneys*. Sports Illustrated

FanNation. https://www.si.com/fannation/name-image-likeness/news/emergence-of-student-athlete-entrepreneurs-creates-new-market-for-attorneys-nick9

Miller, D. (2017). *Building a storybrand : Clarify your message so customers will listen*. Thomas Nelson Pub.

The Mind Tools Content Team. (n.d.). *Win-Win negotiation*. https://www.mindtools.com/ajh8pyd/win-win-negotiation

Mishra, A. (2020, October 26). *Place strategy in marketing mix*. Management Weekly. https://managementweekly.org/place-strategy-in-marketing-mix/

Morales, A. (2023, February 17). Who's behind USC's new NIL collective? Everything you need to know about The Tommy Group. *The Athletic*. https://www.nytimes.com/athletic/4215055/2023/02/16/usc-nil-collective-tommy-group-facts/

Morgan, J. (2019, April 11). *We're going after Nestlé. Here's why*. Greenpeace International. https://www.greenpeace.org/international/story/21712/were-going-after-nestle-heres-why/

Mozafaripour, S. (2019, October 3). *9 popular time management techniques and tools*. University of St. Augustine for Health Sciences. https://www.usa.edu/blog/time-management-techniques/

Mumford, J. (2021, November 5). *9 lessons for becoming a student-athlete entrepreneur*. Lassonde Entrepreneur Institute. https://lassonde.utah.edu/9-lessons-for-becoming-a-student-athlete-entrepreneur/

Murphy, C. B. (2024, May 23). *Understanding the Cash Flow Statement*. Investopedia. https://www.investopedia.com/investing/what-is-a-cash-flow-statement/

Murphy, D. (2021, September 1). *Everything you need to know about the NCAA's NIL debate*. ESPN. https://www.espn.in/college-sports/story/_/id/31086019/everything-need-know-ncaa-nil-debate

Nakos, P. (2022, July 6). *What are NIL collectives and how do they operate?* On3. https://www.on3.com/nil/news/what-are-nil-collectives-and-how-do-they-operate/

Name, image and likeness interim policy resources. (n.d.). NCAA. https://www.ncaa.org/sports/2021/2/8/about-taking-action.aspx

Navigating NCAA compliance: A guide for college athletes. (n.d.). Marygrove College Athletics. https://www.marygrovemustangs.com/navigating-ncaa-compliance-a-guide-for-college-athletes.html

NCAA eligibility center. (n.d.). NCAA. https://web3.ncaa.org/ecwr3/

NCAA name image likeness rule. (2024, May 24). *NCSA College Recruiting*. https://www.ncsasports.org/name-image-likeness

Needle, F. (2020, December 2). *8 ways marketers can leverage social media to meet business objectives*. Blog.hubspot.com. https://blog.hubspot.com/blog/tabid/6307/bid/30888/8-ways-to-leverage-social-media-beyond-social-networks.aspx

NIL collectives database. (n.d.). NIL Newsstand. https://www.nilnewsstand.com/nil-collectives-database

NIL valuations and rankings. (2023). Www.on3.com. https://www.on3.com/nil/rankings/

Njororai Simiyu, W. W. (2010). Individual and institutional challenges facing student athletes on US college campuses. *Journal of Physical Education and Sports Management*, *1*(2), 16–24. https://www.researchgate.net/publication/228336852_Individ

ual_and_institutional_challenges_facing_student_athletes_on_
US_college_campuses

Nozak, W. (2023, July 21). *How to Create a Personal Brand, Monetize Your NIL, and Get Recruited.* Nozak Consulting. https://nozakconsulting.com/branding/how-to-create-a-personal-brand-get-recruited/

Nsouli, E., & King, A. (2022, July 19). *How schools and private entities have engaged in NIL activity.* Sports Shorts. https://www.sports.legal/2022/07/how-schools-and-private-entities-have-engaged-in-nil-activity/

Occhiogrosso, G. (2022, September 26). *10 key points to consider when purchasing A franchise.* Forbes. https://www.forbes.com/sites/garyocchiogrosso/2022/09/26/10-key-points-to-consider-when-purchasing-a-franchise/?sh=790af05c6800

Okkaoglu, O. (2023, March 18). 🚨*Online crisis management: Steps to protect your reputation in the digital age*🚨. LinkedIn. https://www.linkedin.com/pulse/online-crisis-management-steps-protect-your-digital-age-omer-okkaoglu/

Palmeri, S. (2023, May 9). *How NFL draft pick inky johnson never let his career-defining injury define his life.* Goalcast. https://www.goalcast.com/inky-johnson-nfl-draft-pick-injury/

Pattillo, J. L. (2022, October 26). *What do high school recruits need to know about NIL collectives?* Christian Small. https://csattorneys.com/2022/10/26/what-do-high-school-recruits-need-to-know-about-nil-collectives/

Planos, J. (2022, May 16). *The NCAA doesn't know how to stop boosters from playing the NIL game.* FiveThirtyEight. https://fivethirtyeight.com/features/the-ncaa-doesnt-know-how-to-stop-boosters-from-playing-the-nil-game/

Pottinger, M. (2023, February 26). *How a former student athlete set out on an entrepreneurial journey.* The Varsity. https://thevarsity.ca/2023/02/26/how-a-former-student-athlete-set-out-on-an-entrepreneurial-journey/

Priyanka. (2023, December 13). *Revealing Athletic Apparel Market Insights.* Medium. https://medium.com/@priyankapuri0018/revealing-athletic-apparel-market-insights-f767179e4eeb

Ramaswamy, S. (2024, April 26). *The picture-superiority effect: Harness the power of visuals.* Nielsen Norman Group. https://www.nngroup.com/articles/picture-superiority-effect/

Reddy, S. (2024, May 20). *NIL and data transparency: Implications for student-athletes.* Georgetown Law Technology Review. https://georgetownlawtechreview.org/nil-and-data-transparency-implications-for-student-athletes/GLTR-05-2024

Richards, D. J. (n.d.-a). Introducing the "sports marketing mix." *Western Open Books.* https://westernsydney.pressbooks.pub/sportmarketing/chapter/communication-strategy/

Richards, D. J. (n.d.-b). Market segmentation and target marketing in sport. *Western Open Books.* https://westernsydney.pressbooks.pub/sportmarketing/chapter/market-segmentation-and-target-marketing-in-sport/

Romboy, D. (2023, October 10). *How NIL is transforming college sports.* Deseret News. https://www.deseret.com/sports/2023/10/10/23734073/nil-college-football-sports-transform-name-image-likeness-ncaa/

Sanatore, A. (2023, May 9). *Finding the right NIL representation: What to look for in an agent or legal representative.* LinkedIn. https://www.linkedin.com/pulse/finding-right-nil-representation-what-look-agent-legal-sanatore/

Sapkin, G. (2023, April 21). *How student-athletes can monetize their NIL in web3, AI and technology.* LinkedIn. https://www.linkedin.com/pulse/how-student-athletes-can-monetize-nil-web3-ai-grant-sapkin/

Scarborough, H., McAlister, R. (Rosie), & M., P. (n.d.). *How do you use the STAR method to structure your answer to "why should we hire you"?* LinkedIn. https://www.linkedin.com/advice/3/how-do-you-use-star-method-structure-your

Schmidt, J. (n.d.). *Three financial statements.* Corporate Finance Institute. https://corporatefinanceinstitute.com/resources/accounting/three-financial-statements/

Schreck, I. (2022, February 6). *Southern comfort kitchen: Bringing New Orleans style food to Kent on wheels.* KentWired. https://kentwired.com/81912/latest-updates/southern-comfort-kitchen-bringing-new-orleans-style-food-to-kent-on-wheels/

Schultz, A. (2024, January 18). *What percentage of college football players make it to the NFL?* Www.sportskeeda.com. https://www.sportskeeda.com/nfl/what-percentage-college-football-players-make-nfl

Scroggs, L. (2024, April 30). *Time blocking.* Todoist. https://todoist.com/productivity-methods/time-blocking

Sellers, A. (2022, July 21). *What is the buyer's journey?* Hubspot. https://blog.hubspot.com/sales/what-is-the-buyers-journey

Shirey, T. (n.d.). *What Is Online Paid Advertising? (Plus 6 Things to Know).* WebFX Blog. https://www.webfx.com/blog/marketing/online-paid-advertising/

Sibling start-up motus studios is first student-founded clothing brand to partner with U of T. (2024, March 13). University of St. Michael's College. https://stmikes.utoronto.ca/news/sibling-start-up-motus-studios-is-first-student-founded-clothing-brand-to-partner-with-u-of-t

Simplilearn. (2024, February 1). *Business planning: It's importance, types and key elements.* Simplilearn.com. https://www.simplilearn.com/business-planning-article

6 steps to making financial projections for your new business. (2023, February 7). BDC. https://www.bdc.ca/en/articles-tools/start-buy-business/start-business/6-steps-making-financial-projections-new-business

Stubbs, M. (2023, April 23). *Social media and the winning edge: How athletes can harness its power for success.* LinkedIn. https://www.linkedin.com/pulse/social-media-winning-edge-how-athletes-can-harness-its-mathew-stubbs/

Suski, J. (2023, March 31). *Unlocking the secrets of successful brand partnerships.* Brand24. https://brand24.com/blog/successful-brand-partnerships/

Tankimovich, L. (2023, October 23). *12 pros and cons of NIL collectives.* 2aDays . https://www.2adays.com/blog/12-pros-and-cons-of-nil-collectives/

10 powerful qualities of every good marketing expert. (2017, February 6). Grow. https://wearegrow.com/marketing-expert/

Tracy, B. (2017). *Eat that frog! : 21 great ways to stop procrastinating and get more done in less time.* Berrett-Koehler Publishers, Inc., a Bk Life Book. (Original work published 2001)

Transferable skills: Applying athletic skillsets to life after sport. (2023, July 14). Athlete Career Transition.

https://www.athletecareertransition.com/post/transferable-skills-applying-athletic-skillsets-to-life-after-sport

Twain, M. (n.d.). *Mark Twain Quotes.* BrainyQuote. https://www.brainyquote.com/quotes/mark_twain_414009

The 24 character strengths. (n.d.). Via Institute on Character. https://www.viacharacter.org/character-strengths

The ultimate guide to building a robust support network. (2024, April 25). Techtrone. https://www.techtrone.com/how-to-build-a-support-network/

van Schaik, T. (2024, January 1). *5 athlete brand trends.* LinkedIn. https://www.linkedin.com/pulse/6-athlete-brand-trends-thomas-van-schaik-ovele/

Vest, K. (2024, February 14). *Exploring the Athletic Apparel Market Size, Share, Growth, Trends, Innovations, and Consumer Insights.* LinkedIn. https://www.linkedin.com/pulse/exploring-athletic-apparel-market-size-share-growth-trends-kala-vest-fi1tc/

Waddell, C. (2023, December 23). *NIL collectives: How they work and benefit student athletes.* Collage and Wood. https://collageandwood.com/blogs/sports-senior-night/nil-collectives

What does an athletic academic advisor do? (2018, August 20). EKU Online. https://ekuonline.eku.edu/blog/sport/what-does-an-athletic-academic-advisor-do/

What is a business mentor? - The benefits and where to find one. (n.d.). PushFar. https://www.pushfar.com/article/what-is-a-business-mentor-the-benefits-and-where-to-find-one/

What is product strategy? Purpose, fundamentals, types, & steps. (2023, March 10). CoSchedule Blog.

https://coschedule.com/marketing/marketing-mix/product-strategy

Wirth, K. (2024, January 5). *How to come up with a good business idea.* Bplans: Free Business Planning Resources and Templates. https://www.bplans.com/start-a-business/ideas/

Woods, C. (2024, January 19). *10 engaging content ideas for athletes.* LinkedIn. https://www.linkedin.com/pulse/10-engaging-content-ideas-athletes-charlotte-woods-kv4kc/

wowTalkies. (2023, July 15). *Pioneering fan engagement platforms in sports and their unique offerings.* Medium. https://medium.com/@wowTalkies/pioneering-fan-engagement-platforms-in-sports-and-their-unique-offerings-93ba16c439f5

Zhao, M. S. (2020, January 27). *"How I thrive as an athlete turned entrepreneur" with Ellakisha O'Kelley.* Authority Magazine. https://medium.com/authority-magazine/how-i-thrive-as-an-athlete-turned-entrepreneur-with-ellakisha-okelley-f3b9af231da1

www.ingramcontent.com/pod-product-compliance
Lightning Source LLC
Chambersburg PA
CBHW071746150726
47998CB00005B/1830